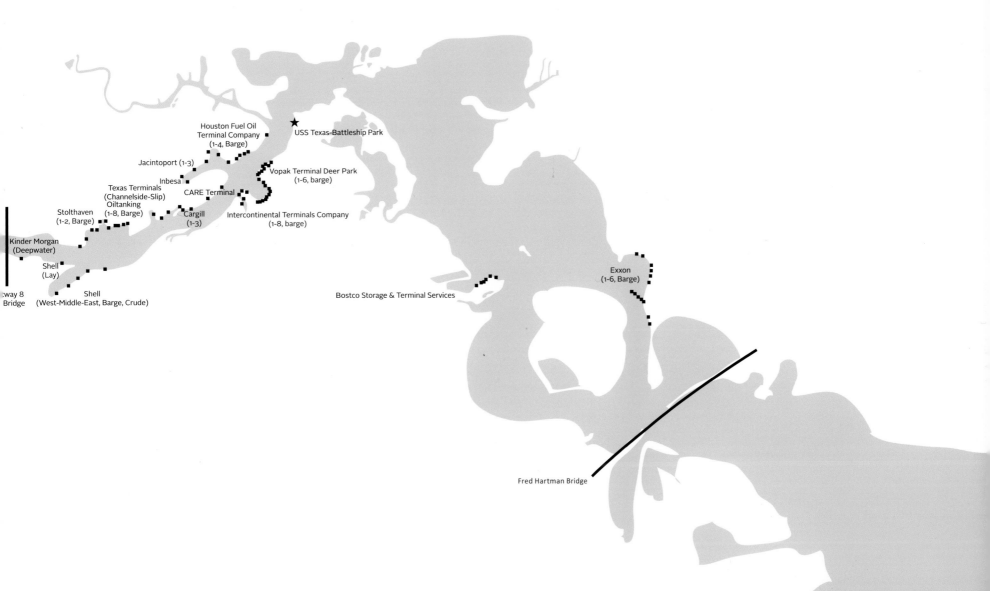

Houston Fuel Oil
Terminal Company
(1-4, Barge)

★ USS Texas-Battleship Park

Jacintoport (1-3)

Vopak Terminal Deer Park
(1-6, barge)

Inbesa

Texas Terminals
(Channelside-Slip)   CARE Terminal
Oiltanking
(1-8, Barge)

Stolthaven
(1-2, Barge)   Cargill
                         (1-3)   Intercontinental Terminals Company
                                    (1-8, barge)

Kinder Morgan
(Deepwater)

Shell
(Lay)

Exxon
(1-6, Barge)

way 8   Shell
Bridge   (West-Middle-East, Barge, Crude)   Bostco Storage & Terminal Services

Fred Hartman Bridge

PORT OF HOUSTON'S ECONOMIC IMPACT

- 1 million jobs in statewide
- 2.1 million jobs nationwide
- $179 billion statewide
- $499 billion nationwide
- $4.5 billion tax revenue statewide
- $52.1 billion tax revenue nationwide
- 13.3% of export tonnage in U.S. (#2)
- 10.4% of import tonnage in U.S. (#1)

LINKING THE WORLD TO HOUSTON
AND HOUSTON TO THE WORLD

Dear Friends,

I have often said that a good idea powered by effective partnership knows no limit. Consider the Houston Ship Channel and the Port of Houston.

The Port of Houston had humble beginnings in the 19th century, when cotton and lumber were barged to Galveston and then loaded onto deep-draft vessels for eventual transport to other markets. Today, the Port of Houston is the No. 1 port in the nation in foreign tonnage. This is a stunning achievement.

The bold vision of our own citizenry and their relentless dedication brought into being a deep-water port for Houston. Although the idea had little more than local support for many years, with the Great Storm of 1900 that destroyed Galveston, the discovery of oil at Spindletop in 1901, and growing demand for cotton, lumber, and other crops, a deep-water channel linking Houston to ready markets for Texas bounty gained traction.

However, there was still the thorny problem of funding this massive project, a 52-mile deep-water channel from Houston to the Gulf of Mexico. A novel idea, again conceived by local visionaries, soon solved that problem. For the first time in the history of a federal waterway, local citizens agreed to partner with the federal government and pay half of the cost of dredging the deep-water channel. Impressed with the idea that local citizens would share that cost, Congress approved what came to be known as the "Houston Plan," and the Houston Ship Channel was opened on November 10, 1914.

From that great vision and partnership, in less than a century, the Houston Ship Channel became home to the largest petrochemical complex in the nation, and the second largest in the world; Houston has grown to be the fourth largest city and premier metropolitan export region in the nation, and a thriving metropolis with a growing economy that is the envy of cities around the country. Because of the industry along the Houston Ship Channel, our state-of-the-art infrastructure, and ready access to foreign markets, Texas has been the No. 1 state for exports for 12 consecutive years, and the Port of Houston contributes more than $178 billion of economic impact and more than 1 million jobs in Texas alone. The Houston Ship Channel was the genesis of the industry that has proliferated along the channel, and is a huge driver of our economy and continued prosperity.

The first century of this achievement has been remarkable indeed. As we celebrate the 100-year anniversary of the Houston Ship Channel in this year 2014, it is appropriate to remember the great legacy that has been entrusted to us—a legacy that has fueled our economy for 100 years and will drive our expansion through the next century.

We owe a huge debt of gratitude to those that came before us. Let's continue to dream and fully embrace the unlimited possibility of our future. Together, in partnership, we can continue this legacy of success for generations to come.

Janiece Longoria

Janiece M. Longoria, Chairman, The Port of Houston Authority

100

Photographers:
David Bray, Chris Kuhlman, Jim Olive Photography, and special thanks to Lou Vest

Photographs courtesy of:
Bay-IBI Group Architects courtesy of San Jacinto College,
Gilbreath Communications, Inc., Greater Houston Port Bureau,
©Houston Chronicle, Judson Design, Port of Houston Archives,
Hoerr Schaudt with White Oak Studio courtesy of Hermann Park Conservancy,
and Tellepsen Family Archives

We would like to thank all of the people who gave their time, talent and energy to bring this book to publication.

Designed by:
Limb Design, Houston, Texas

Printed by:
Bayside Printing, Houston, Texas

ISBN # 978-0-692-24309-1
Library of Congress

In the making of this book, every attempt has been made to verify names, facts and figures.

The paper used in the printing of this book is grown in and harvested from managed forests.

FSC
MIX
Paper
FSC® C004628

THIS BOOK IS MADE POSSIBLE BY THESE GENEROUS CONTRIBUTORS

EXXONMOBIL

CENTERPOINT ENERGY

HOUSTON PILOTS

KIRBY CORPORATION

PORT OF HOUSTON AUTHORITY

BUFFALO MARINE SERVICE, INC.

DANNENBAUM ENGINEERING CORPORATION

GREATER HOUSTON PORT BUREAU

GREATER HOUSTON CONVENTION AND VISITORS BUREAU

GULF WINDS INTERNATIONAL, INC.

HOUSTON ARTS ALLIANCE

INTERCONTINENTAL TERMINALS COMPANY

INTERNATIONAL LONGSHOREMEN'S ASSOCIATION

KORNEGAY AND COMPANY, LLC

MORAN SHIPPING AGENCIES, INC.

NOLAN AND BOBBIE RICHARDSON FAMILY

SHELL OIL COMPANY

JACOB STERN & SONS, INC.

TELLEPSEN FAMILY

VOPAK

TABLE OF CONTENTS

100

THIS BOOK CHRONICLES THE PAST 100 YEARS OF HOUSTON'S DEEP-WATER PORT

2014

AND THE ASTOUNDING EFFORTS TO HOLD ON TO THAT DREAM—AND MAKE IT GROW.

Just about every hour, a blue-water ship enters or leaves the Houston Ship Channel at Bolivar Point—8,300 ship movements per year on the Port of Houston. Many of those vessels carry the nearly 2 million containers handled by the Barbours Cut and Bayport Terminals north of Kemah. Other ships push up into the channel and stop at one of the private terminals along Buffalo Bayou. Some navigate all the way up to the Turning Basin and wharves just inside the 610 East Loop.

THIS IS THE HOUSTON SHIP CHANNEL

The Port story is born along with the City of Houston in 1836, but 2014 marks the centennial of the achievement of a long held dream—that Houston become a deep-water port where vessels could transport cargo directly to and from other nations, with no stops in between. Initially, Buffalo Bayou was the "slow boat" to development—an underdog in the race to become a major commercial artery. Without the Houston Ship Channel, carved from the very shallows of Buffalo Bayou, "the town that built a port that built a city" might never have existed as it is today. It was the classic American humorist Will Rogers who best summed up the spirit of Houstonians when he said, "Houston dared to dig a ditch, and bring the sea to its door."

Perhaps it was the kind of person attracted to the bayou area—many of the early settlers had the grit and wherewithal to withstand the climate, the unforgiving environment, the outbreaks of malaria and yellow fever, and the ever-present threat of sometimes hostile natives and often ruthless brigands. Through it all, there was something that called to them, that made them look at that slow moving, dark water creek in a way no one else would or should have predicted. They didn't see a bayou. They didn't see a possibility. They saw inevitability.

It was a hard fought process that started with men using axes to clear land, building wharves by hand, and with man-powered dredging vessels to drag muck from the sandy bottom bayou. Cargo on barges and shallow draft steamers began flowing to the Gulf from the foot of Main Street in Houston. Eventually, steam power came into play, and the bayou became a channel—wider, deeper, and straighter so that larger vessels could work their way up to the Houston railhead. Cotton, timber, and molasses, followed by the discovery of the East Texas oilfields, would nurture the dream of a deep-water port in Houston.

Allen Brothers hired Gail Borden to lay out streets starting at the south bank of Buffalo Bayou. This is the plan. Borden later became famous for his condensed milk.

THE TOWN OF HOUSTON.

SITUATED at the head of navigation, on the West bank of Buffalo Bayou, is now for the first time brought to public notice because, until now, the proprietors were not ready to offer it to the public, with the advantages of capital and improvements.

The town of Houston is located at a point on the river which must ever command the trade of the largest and richest portion of Texas. By reference to the map, it will be seen that the trade of San Jacinto, Spring Creek, New Kentucky and the Brazos, above and below Fort Bend, must necessarily come to this place, and will at this time warrant the employment of at least ONE MILLION DOLLARS of capital, and when the rich lands of this country shall be settled, a trade will flow to it, making it, beyond all doubt, the great interior commercial emporium of Texas.

The town of Houston is distant 15 miles from the Brazos river, 30 miles, a little North of East, from San Felippe, 60 miles from Washington, 40 miles from Lake Creek, 30 miles South West from New Kentucky, and 15 miles by water and 8 or 10 by land above Harrisburg. Tide water runs to this place and the lowest depth of water is about six feet. Vessels from New Orleans or New York can sail without obstacle to this place, and steamboats of the largest class can run down to Galveston Island in 8 or 10 hours, in all seasons of the year. It is but a few hours sail down the bay, where one may take an excursion of pleasure and enjoy the luxuries of fish, fowl, oysters and sea bathing. Galveston harbor being the only one in which vessels drawing a large draft of water can navigate, must necessarily render the Island the great naval and commercial depot of the country.

The town of Houston must be the place where arms, amunitions and provisions for the government will be stored, because, situated in the very heart of the country, it combines security and the means of easy distribution, and a national armory will no doubt very soon be established at this point.

There is no place in Texas more healthy, having an abundance of excellent spring water, and enjoying the sea breeze in all its freshness. No place in Texas possesses so many advantages for building, having Pine, Ash, Cedar and Oak in inexhaustible quantities; also the tall and beautiful Magnolia grows in abundance. In the vicinity are fine quarries of stone.

Nature appears to have designated this place for the future seat of Government. It is handsome and beautifully elevated, salubrious and well watered, and now in the very heart or centre of population, and will be so for a length of time to come. It combines two important advantages: a communication with the coast and foreign countries, and with the different portions of the Republic. As the country shall improve, rail roads will become in use, and will be extended from this point to the Brazos, and up the same, also from this up to the head waters of San Jacinto, embracing that rich country, and in a few years the whole trade of the upper Brazos will make its way into Galveston Bay through this channel.

Preparations are now making to erect a water Saw Mill, and a large Public House for accommodation, will soon be opened. Steamboats now run in this river, and will in a short time commence running regularly to the Island.

The proprietors offer the lots for sale on moderate terms to those who desire to improve them, and invite the public to examine for themselves.

A. C. ALLEN, for
A. C. & J. K. ALLEN.

August 30, 1836.—6m

The Commercial Bulletin, of New Orleans, Mobile Advertiser, the Globe, at Washington, Morning Courier and New York Enquirer, New York Herald, and Louisville Public Advertiser are requested to make three insertions of this advertisement, and forward their bills to this office for payment.

"THE IRIDESCENT DREAM" – A DEEP-WATER PORT

Augustus and John Allen landed at the junction of White Oak and Buffalo Bayou, referring to the location as "in the midst of a sylvan retreat, where the song of the birds and the whisper of the breeze were the only sounds to be heard." This early photograph shows Buffalo Bayou as it might have been seen by the Allen Brothers as they imagined its future.

1836

Texas Independence from Mexico

1836

Brothers Augustus Chapman Allen and John
Kirby Allen found Houston

1836

Houston becomes temporary capital of Texas

The first recorded ship call to Houston occurred in January 1837 when the steamboat Laura sailed up Buffalo Bayou.

The *Laura* is widely accepted as the first commercial vessel to visit Houston's port. At that time the Port was a cut through a bluff on the banks of Buffalo Bayou at the foot of Main Street in the tent town of Houston, Texas. The *Laura* is important because she was to navigate Buffalo Bayou as a fairly sizable paddle wheeler. A passenger of note on the *Laura* was Francis R. Lubbock, future governor of Texas.

FOR THE CITY OF HOUSTON.
THE REGULAR
PACKET STEAMER
LAURA,
T. W. GRAYSON, MASTER.
WILL leave Marion, on Tuesday, the 21st February, at 4 o'clock, P. M. for the above city, and all intermediate ports. For freight or passage apply on board; or to Aldridge and Davis, Marion, or to Thomas H. Borden. Columbia.
N. B.—The Laura, this trip, will touch at Anahuac.
Columbia, Feb. 20, 1837.   59-1

Houston 1856 (approximate population 4,500) at the foot of Main Street with the sternwheeler, St. Clair.

1837
The *Laura* was the first steamship on Buffalo Bayou

SAN JACINTO BATTLEGROUND

In 1856 the Texas Veteran's Association began lobbying the state legislature to create a memorial to the men who died during the Texas Revolution. The legislature made no efforts to commemorate the final battle of the revolution until the 1890s, when funds were finally appropriated to purchase the land where the Battle of San Jacinto took place. After a careful survey to determine the boundaries of the original battle site, land was purchased for a new state park east of Houston in 1897. This became the San Jacinto Battleground State Historic Site.

The San Jacinto Battleground entry before the monument was built.

Taken around 1873, this photograph shows the freight boat, Lizzie, a side-wheeler operated by the Houston Direct Navigation Company, being loaded with cotton at the Houston docks.
She may have also carried passengers. On the opposite bank of Buffalo Bayou, barges are stacked with cargo and ready for railroad cars.

1840

Wharf built from Main to Fannin

1841

City ordinance establishing Port of
Houston

1845

Texas becomes the 28th state in
the Union

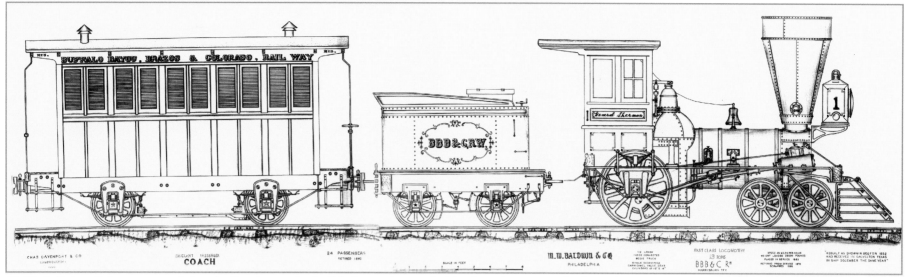

M. W. Baldwin and Company, provided early advertisement for Buffalo Bayou, Brazos & Colorado Railway. General Sidney Sherman (610 Bridge's namesake) and prominent Houston and Galveston men completed this railway to the Brazos by 1852, making it the first railroad of Texas.

As an alternative to exorbitant shipping fees from Galveston, Commodore John Morgan cut the land at Morgan's Point to dredge the first channel to Buffalo Bayou in 1876, changing the direction from a river port to a seaport. However, his lofty status with Port supporters soon dissipated when he installed a heavy chain to ensure toll payment for water passage.

Hauling timber pre-1900s on the Southern Pacific Railroad. John Henry Kirby was a businessman whose ventures made him arguably the largest lumber manufacturer in Texas and the southern United States. With his successful reputation, he would be known by his business peers as "The Prince of the Pines."

Entrepreneurs will tell you that achieving success isn't about getting there—it's staying there. That is the challenge. Keeping Houston's deep-water dream alive required exactly the same perseverance as achieving it in the first place. It involved overcoming two World Wars, the Great Depression, the furies of nature, and the doubts of man. The Port of Houston is a success because Houstonians had a vision then, and we see it continue today—a modern port vital not just to Houston, not just to Texas, but to the United States. The Port of Houston is ranked as number two in the United States by total tonnage (ranked first in foreign tonnage and second in overall tonnage for 18 consecutive years) and cargo value—a ranking fed by numerous and massive vessels carrying freight to and from all corners of the world. Each year, those 8,300 blue-water ships visit the Port of Houston, generating 20,400 ship movements just within the port itself. Barges moving fuel, general and break-bulk cargo account for another 200,000 movements. These astounding numbers likely have exceeded even the wildest expectations of early port visionaries.

One of the first steam sawmills in Texas was planned in 1829 in what is now modern Houston. After the Texas Revolution, lumber production increased steadily and by 1860 there were reportedly 200 saw mills in the state. The construction of railroads throughout the eastern part of the state led to a boom in lumber production starting in the 1880s.

Timber was big business in Texas, nearly equal to cotton. Old growth trees were felled and often floated down Buffalo Bayou and San Jacinto River to various mills along their banks (Circa 1900).

HOUSTON, WHERE 17 RAILROADS MEET THE SEA

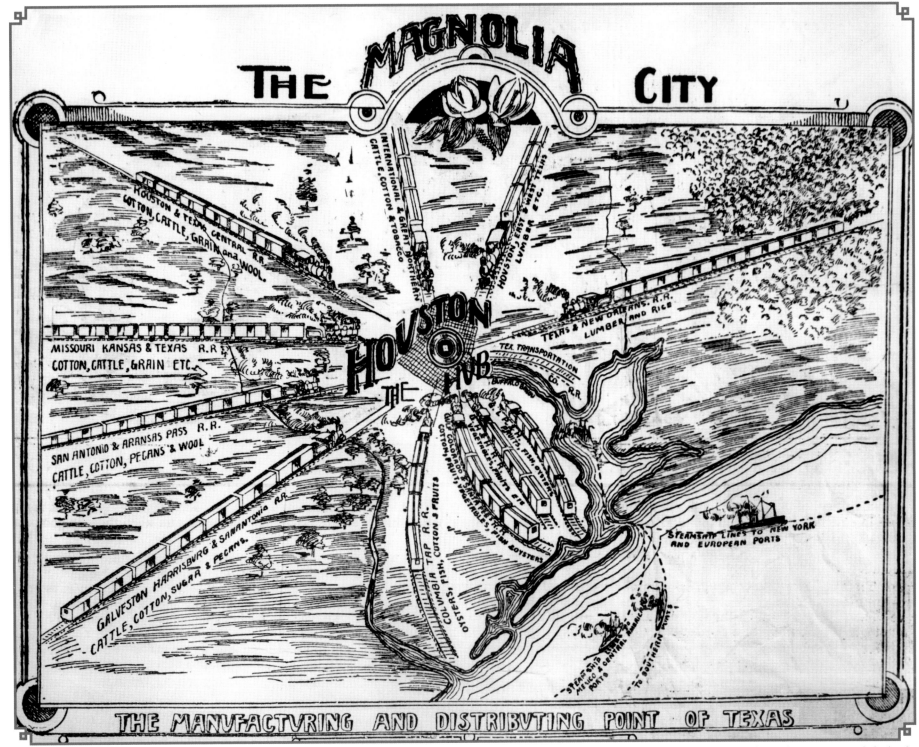

Houston, "The Magnolia City," is promoted in this early advertisement as "The Hub" of manufacturing and distribution by rail and sea. As early as the eve of the Civil War, Houston had already established itself as the railroad center of Texas. After the war, development was rapid. By 1880, 2,200 miles of track were laid in Texas and 1,800 of it led to Houston. In 1910, 17 railroads connected to Houston, and the 18th was added in 1927.

1870
Congress designates Houston
a port

1876
The *Clinton* was the first ocean steamship to call

1895
Houston receives heaviest snowfall on record.
Over 20 inches buries the city and does not
melt for days

COTTON, KING OF COMMERCE AND TRADE

"Cotton is king!" This expression accurately described commerce along Buffalo Bayou during this era and the transport to multiple railroads.

Barges, like the one above, whose picture was taken in 1899, were a constant sight along Buffalo Bayou. Cotton bales were handled from the moment they arrived in Houston, and then processed in compresses to be ferried downstream to ships. At every step there were tolls, fees, and charges—a percentage of which often went to maintain the bayou. Final destination for this load was Boston, via the steamship Catania.

1896

Tom Ball begins term as congressman

1896

Congress Rivers and Harbors Committee approves survey of Houston Ship Channel from Galveston Island to Houston

1899

Houston's first park opens. The site, now Sam Houston Park, contains several of Houston's earliest buildings

The Cotton Exchange Building, circa 1900, symbolizes the force of cotton in the drive to create a Port of Houston. Cotton was one of Houston's chief export products; among others were timber, flour, and sugar. Cotton's supremacy would eventually be replaced with the discovery of oil in East Texas.

Loading "White Gold" at the Bayou City Cotton Compress in the 1890s.

Buffalo Bayou has another peculiar advantage — unlike most significant Texas streams, it flows almost due east and west. With the Brazos River extending in a general northerly direction, this meant that the head of navigation on the bayou was but 20 miles or so from the heart of the fertile agricultural region of the Brazos.

— HISTORIAN ANDREW FOREST MUIR, 1958

COTTON ON THE SHIP CHANNEL, HOUSTON, TEXAS
SHIPMENTS AMOUNT TO NEARLY 400000 BALES PER YEAR.

As the sun set on the nineteenth century, Galveston was considered the gem of Texas. Her nicknames were "Ellis Island of the West," "Venice of the Gulf," and even the "Wall Street of the South." In 1899, Galveston boasted a population of 37,000 residents to Houston's 27,500, and had more millionaires per capita than any other U.S. city during the era. Galveston also had the advantage of a natural harbor with easy access to the Gulf of Mexico, making it a trade center for Texas and on par with New Orleans—and Houston's primary adversary for trade.

In the mid-1890s, legislation made it through Congress that would result in a thorough survey for a channel to Houston. However, it required a visit from the Congressional Rivers and Harbors Committee before final approval. Ordinarily, that would have been fine, but 1896 was a very dry year, and Buffalo Bayou at the foot of Main Street Houston wasn't much more than a brook. Having just been elected to the House of Representatives, Thomas H. Ball, the freshman from Texas, was nervous. In February of 1897, the committee was on their way to Houston, and Buffalo Bayou was nearly as dry as a wagon rut.

There's an old saying: "I'd rather be lucky than smart any day." And again, Houston got lucky. Seemingly on cue, a winter front blew into town and brought a gully-washer. Buffalo Bayou's level surged five feet over its banks by the time the Washington dignitaries arrived for inspection.

In true Texas fashion, residents opened their homes to guests who were lavishly entertained with the finest food and spirits Houston had to offer. The delegation was carefully guided on a select tour route that put Houston and the bayou in the best light, and included the hallowed grounds of San Jacinto Battleground. It's also said that longtime Buffalo Bayou booster, Eber W. Cave, practiced a little slight of hand whilst cruising with the committee on the bayou. Cave was taking soundings as they went downstream—for the benefit of his special audience, he called out somewhat exaggerated depths without letting the guests see the markings on the line.

100

Elegant estates like the one above at Vick's Park, near the present cloverleaf at Allen Parkway, were located on the banks of Buffalo Bayou in the 1900s. Later in the 1920s, Houstonians flocked to the natural banks along the waters for recreation in the form of picnics, canoeing, and regattas. That legacy continues today as various parks and green spots are preserved for picnics, jogging, biking, and biking.

The summer of 1896 brought congressional approval for a detailed survey and estimates, not only for the original request of the bayou from Harrisburg to Houston, but also from the docks of Houston all the way to the tip of Bolivar—far more than had been hoped. The survey team split the channel into three parts— Bolivar to Morgan's Point Canal, Morgan's Point to Harrisburg, and Harrisburg to Houston. Dredging the first two legs of the channel from Bolivar to Morgan's Point to Harrisburg would be relatively simple, although the leg to Harrisburg would entail various land rights-of-way. The last leg, however, would be very difficult and far too expensive. This was due to the high banks of the bayou and additional rights-of-way. Nevertheless, engineers supported the general idea of improvement to the channel.

While Houston was ready to get down to the business of carving out the channel, a political foe muddied up matters. Representative Theodore Burton from Ohio decided that the deep-water channel for Houston was impractical. His decision was important because he became the head of the Rivers and Harbors Committee when the previous chair resigned to take another position. Burton's opposition was based not on the survey as a whole, but on the problematic leg between Harrisburg and the foot of Main Street in Houston. Fortunately, Congressman Thomas Ball, who succeeded fellow Texan Joseph C. Hutcheson, the person responsible for the 1896 Port survey, did not stray from his purpose. The early appropriations were small but they were a start. Then providence took a hand.

Then as now, area residents used Buffalo Bayou for recreation. This image shows picnickers near the San Jacinto Battleground, celebrating Texas Independence Day.

1900
City of Houston population at 63,800

THE 1900 STORM

Like Atlantis, the gem of the south was washed from the map in a single night. Hammering winds up to 143 miles per hour pushed a 15-foot storm surge across the island, wiping out nearly every structure in its path and taking the lives of an estimated 8,000 people. On September 9, 1900, the city of Galveston no longer existed.

Commonly referred to as the "1900 Storm," many Houstonians believe this was the single driving force behind the success of Houston's deep-water project. But substantial funding did not follow the storm as some might expect. The storm proved the point that a protected harbor and inland port would better serve commerce, but the chairman of the Rivers and Harbors Committee still opposed Houston as the site. Burton simply thought it an impractical solution. Undeterred, Representative Ball executed some political maneuvers with his fellow committee members, resulting in a coalition of backers to override Burton for a funding vote in 1902. Significant appropriations emerged from the unwavering efforts of the congressman from Texas, as well as from the boosters back home with the Houston Cotton Exchange. Deep-water was within sight.

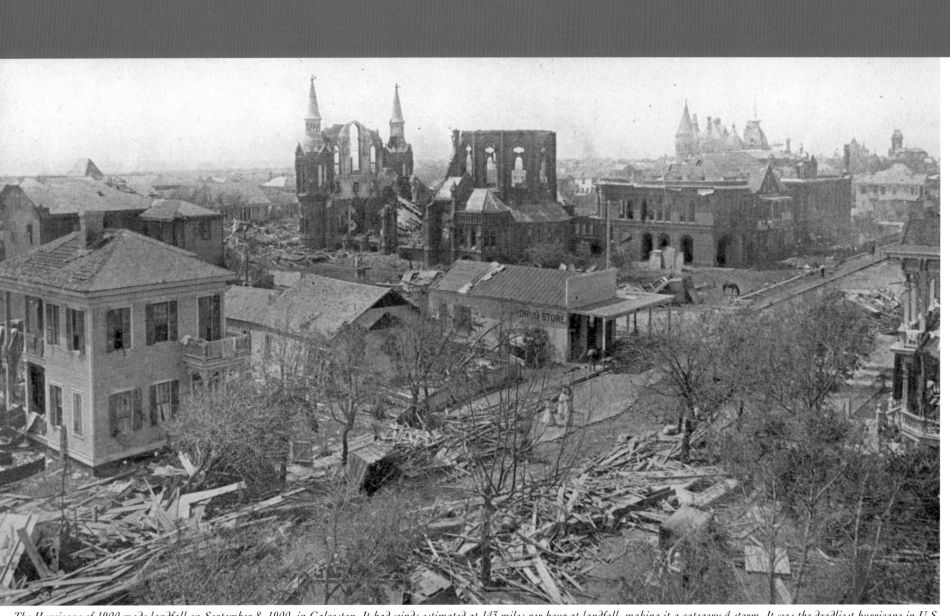

The Hurricane of 1900 made landfall on September 8, 1900, in Galveston. It had winds estimated at 143 miles per hour at landfall, making it a category 4 storm. It was the deadliest hurricane in U.S. history causing great loss of life with the estimated death toll cited in official reports as 8,000. Because of this natural disaster, Galveston's reputation as "the Great Commercial Emporium" was ended.

1900

Great Storm devastates
Galveston Island

Buffalo Bayou generated "Main Street" commerce.

1901

First oil gusher comes in at Spindletop

1902

Congress appropriates dredging
funds for Houston Ship Channel

1903

Wright Brothers first to fly

SPINDLETOP LAUNCHES AN ERA OF OIL

On January 10, 1901, heavy oil spouted 200 feet into the air in the greatest gusher Americans had ever seen.

Oil derricks dominated the prairie landscape.

The Texas Oil Boom was a period of dramatic change and economic growth during the early 20th century that began with the discovery of Spindletop, a large petroleum reserve near Beaumont, Texas. This discovery ushered in an era in which oil would quickly catch up to cotton as one of Houston's chief exports. Within a few decades, cotton would take a back seat.

1907
Channel dredged to 18.5' depth

1909
Houston Plan adopted by Congress
to finance channel improvements

1911
Harris County Houston Ship Channel Navigation District created

CHANNELING THE BAYOU

By 1904, much of the channel through Galveston Bay had been completed. Work was well underway on the lower portion of the second leg above Morgan's Point and in the canal through it. The project was progressing smoothly, though not quickly, and costs had risen since the original 1896 survey that led to congressional approval of the first dredging activity of substantial consequence to an 18.5 foot channel depth. What's more, these costs brought back into sharp focus the fuzzy question of just how far up Buffalo Bayou the project should extend: to the original head of navigation at Harrisburg, or all the way up that long and winding bayou to downtown Houston. The reality that every Houstonian knew but was reluctant to admit was that the upper Buffalo Bayou would have to be totally altered to allow the ever-increasing size of vessels. The natural course was just too narrow and serpentine to make the price tag feasible. Houston had also expanded, occupying much of the area under consideration for a turning basin and it took extensive discussion to settle on Constitution Bend as the location for the Turning Basin at Long Reach. Nevertheless, the site was designated and, following two years of work, the Turning Basin was completed in 1908. Later, the city built two slips for accommodating large vessels.

In the meantime, work continued at other points leading to the bay. It's worth noting that progress was facilitated because many landowners allowed generous rights-of-way on their properties along the banks. Their inspiration was in part from pride at the fruition of a long-held dream. Part of it, too, was purely commercial, knowing that land values would rise along the channel as industry was attracted to the area. An illustrative case was Southern Pacific, which donated 15 acres of land to make way for a cut—acreage that had facilities on it. The company removed those facilities without ever presenting a bill for the land or requesting compensation. In other cases, those who could—individuals and companies or organizations—donated land as needed. If an owner could not afford to donate land, a group of citizens sometimes banded together to buy the tract at a fair rate and in turn donated the right-of-way to the government.

Since the Rivers and Harbors Committee vote in 1902, much had been accomplished, but even more needed to be done before the new deep-water Port of Houston could open. Sometimes work was held up by contract adjustments due to higher costs. After all, along the lower Buffalo Bayou, there were a couple of bends that needed to be straightened out—literally. And then there was the widening of the course and disposing of the resulting dredge spoils. Despite the generosity of the donors for rights-of-way, legal and bureaucratic processes still had to be satisfied. It didn't help when there was a hiccup in the national economy from 1910 to 1912.

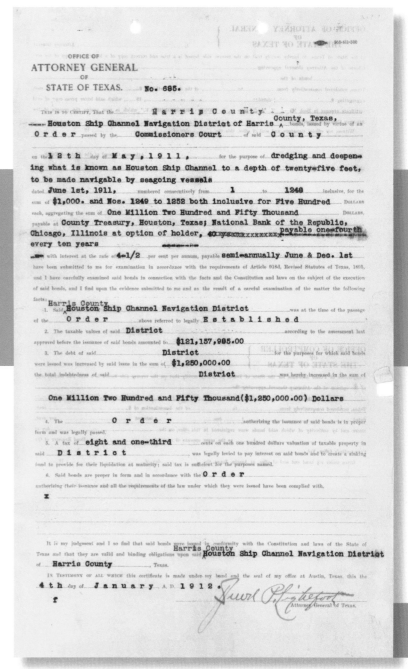

This is one of the bond documents issued by the Harris County Houston Ship Channel Navigation District (today's Port of Houston Authority) in 1912 for the purpose of dredging the channel so that vessels with deeper drafts could steam up to the port. Local business leaders convinced Houstonians that improvements to the port and the channel were paramount to their success, and therefore, the bonds were necessary.

1911

"Houston Plan" Bond approved by 16-1 margin

The Washington *(below) and* Pensacola *(above) were two of a handful of dredges working on the Houston Ship Channel in 1912. Dredging was completed a year ahead of schedule in September 1914.*

This 1914 photograph may be one of the last images of the port that was originally at the foot of Main Street in Houston.

100

Patrol boat in the early days of the Port of Houston.

Photo by Geo. Beach.

MAIN STREET VIADUCT AND SHIP CHANNEL, HOUSTON, TEXAS.

Main span of Houston's "half million dollar" Main Street Viaduct of 1,300 feet. The bridge, built in 1911 at Allen's Landing, connected the north and south sides of Houston with the Southern Pacific Building in the right background.

1912

Houston Ship Channel route altered

1912

Titanic sinks

1912

Rice Institute founded

Horace Baldwin Rice, nephew of Rice University founder William Marsh Rice, was a major proponent of a deep-water port for Houston. It's said that he used no small portion of his own wealth to foster interest, support, and investment in anything advancing the realization of the Port of Houston. He was also a five-term mayor of Houston during the primary work on the Houston Ship Channel. By 1904 Federal funding of $1,000,000 had been exhausted in attempting to widen the channel and reach an 18.5 foot depth to the head of Long Reach. Things needed to keep moving and once again funding was at the top of the list, whether it be federal and/or by another source.

In early 1909, Rice mobilized his port allies and a plan quickly took shape. Simply stated, Houston needed a mechanism to raise funds to reach a 25 foot channel depth to open the Port to the world including anticipated increased traffic from the nearly complete Panama Canal and to accommodate larger ships. Since most of the ship channel was outside the city limits, it was also outside the city's authority. Thomas Ball, no longer in Congress by this time, suggested creating a governing body over the entire channel operating area. It would be called a navigation district and its headquarters would be seated in Houston. Authorization for such a district had to come in two parts. The first was through the state of Texas legislature, which had the power to create special districts to manage waterways and related resources. Ball's congressional experience made him Rice's natural choice to head the team responsible for lobbying lawmakers. The team would also align their efforts with those of other Texas coastal cities chasing after deep-water. By mid 1909, legislation provided for the creation of Navigation Districts. The second part of authorizing the navigation district had to come from voter approval. Convincing people in different communities along the channel to relinquish authority over the channel took some special promoting, especially since some citizens had little interest or weren't within proximity of the project to gain financially. Most importantly at that time, the fund-raising mechanism would be in place through the Navigation District's authority to issue bonds to raise money for waterway maintenance and improvements—the long awaited completion of the 25-foot channel depth project.

Here is where the brilliance of Thomas Ball is exemplified.

An astute politician, Ball knew two things unquestionably. One was that voters were going to look sideways at the idea of issuing over a million dollars of debt to complete the project. Second, with rising costs on the channel, Ball also knew that Congress had bitten off more than it liked chewing, particularly as the national economy was showing signs of trouble. Therefore, Ball initiated a strategy that included Washington. He proposed that the new district, and thereby the voters, share half the cost of completing the work the federal government had started. The offer by Port proponents and his deep-water committee was the first time in U.S. history that a locality committed to guarantee a contribution of funds to a federal project. This method of shared funding has since become the standard. Certain conditions applied, but the Rivers and Harbors Committee unanimously approved of the "Houston Plan." Then, the campaign to convince voters began.

Thomas Henry Ball (1859 – 1944) was a Texas politician and a Democratic member of the United States House of Representatives. Thomas Henry Ball and Frank Andrews formed a law firm in Houston in 1902.

Melvin Kurth joined in 1913. Ball's Houston law practice represented chiefly railroads and corporations, and he promoted Texas port facilities both in Congress and back in Houston. He served as the first general counsel for the Navigation District after its founding.

Because Ball had been instrumental in routing a railroad through Peck, Texas, the town was renamed Tomball, Texas in his honor in 1907.

1913
Houston Symphony established

1914
Hermann Park opens

1914
USS Texas is launched

Horace Baldwin Rice was a prominent early Texas businessman. Rice was also very active in politics, serving once as Harris County commissioner and five times as mayor of Houston, from 1896 to 1898 and again from 1905 to 1913. He was also the grandson of Horace Baldwin, who served as the Houston mayor in 1844.

The yacht, Zeeland, owned by H. Baldwin Rice, mayor of Houston and nephew of William Marsh Rice, was used to show visitors the Houston Ship Channel at his expense.

Original Rice Hotel

Rebuilt Rice Hotel

This is the view of downtown Houston with the Rice Hotel as it appeared circa 1900. Jesse Jones, Houston's noted businessman, would raze this structure and erect the iconic "E" shaped building of today. At this time, downtown traffic still consisted mostly of old-fashioned horsepower, as opposed to newfangled automobiles, two of which are seen parked in front of the hotel. It was around this same time, in 1906, that the last purported gunfight in front of the original hotel took place. Evidence is scant, but numerous editorials in Houston papers from the same period supported a citywide ban on carrying sidearms (population approximately 60,000).

As the work progressed to organize and establish what would become the Harris County Houston Ship Channel Navigation District, politicians, business leaders, and civic organizations went about gathering support for voter approval. Town hall meetings were often contentious, but inspired oratory often shamed opponents as being almost unpatriotic. In 1911, voters went to the polls. In Houston, Mayor Rice declared a half-day holiday so that the electorate would turn out. The voters overwhelmingly approved the measure, and soon after, the Harris County Houston Ship Channel Navigation District began issuing bonds. At first the bonds were a flop with the public and bankers. For the bankers, it was a matter of low commissions and price restrictions as dictated by law.

Enter Jesse H. Jones.

Jones was a powerhouse. He knew just about anyone who was anyone in Houston. The Jones' empire eventually included construction, real estate, news publishing, lumber, and banking. It was the latter that came in handy with the bonds. Within 24 hours of meeting with Mayor Rice to discuss the bond crisis, Jones secured commitments from almost every bank in Houston to purchase them and fund Houston's share of the channel dredge work. Granted, many of the bank presidents were port supporters, but when they were reluctant to follow words with funds, Jones helped firm up their resolve.

JESSE H. JONES

Jesse Jones (1874–1956) was one of the gems in the triple crown of giants in the 1914 chapter of the Port of Houston. Along with Horace Rice and Thomas Ball, he was a driving force in convincing bankers, Congress, and Houstonians that money should be spent to improve the channel and establish the Port of Houston as it is known today. Jones, a powerhouse businessman, served in Franklin Roosevelt's cabinet, and as Chairman of the Reconstruction Finance Corporation, helped rebuild America's economy during the Depression. Houston Endowment Inc. was founded in 1937 by Jesse H. Jones and Mary Gibbs Jones as an extension of their personal philanthropy to establish institutions and organizations that helped facilitate the growth of Houston and develop its people. It was the principal beneficiary of Jesse and Mary Jones' estates after their deaths. In addition to his role as "Financier of the Port," Jones changed the Houston skyline, including two city landmarks— the Neils Esperson Building and the Rice Hotel.

100

A FAMILIAR SIGHT: Ongoing dredging and widening of the Houston Ship Channel. In 1908 dredging operations were completed in a wide natural bend in the bayou, an ideal spot for the Turning Basin, increasing the diameter from 600 to 1,100 feet.

Captain W.L. Farnsworth brought the Dorothy, *a vessel drawing 19 feet of water, down the Houston Ship Channel with 3,000 pounds of anthracite coal from Philadelphia and was unloaded by a floating derrick at Clinton in October 1914 which was one month before the Port officially opened. In 1974, a Port Authority fireboat was named after Captain Farnsworth.*

Everything looked as if it were falling into place—support, financing, and progress on the channel. Even the city of Houston, for its part, issued bonds to add new port projects while improving existing facilities, and established a harbor board to manage them. Then it was discovered that crosscurrents in the bay were filling in the channel and shoaling. Engineers proposed moving the channel slightly to a western route where the currents were less severe. In addition, they recommended using the dredge material to create islands as a barrier against currents. That island string exists today and connects with Atkinson Island, presently a beneficial use site for bird nesting and marsh growth. The adjusted route was completed on September 7, 1914, with the final work ahead of schedule by a year. On that morning, the dredge *Texas* signaled by a ceremonial whistle the completion of the channel and the subsequent removal of 25 million cubic yards of dredged material.

Houstonians planned a monumental and well-deserved celebration to mark the opening of the Port of Houston. There were galas, pageants, parades, and all manner of festivities. Houston's deep-water port was now ready for great oceangoing vessels. It was a dream dating back to the Allen brothers when they founded Houston. The celebration culminated on November 10, 1914, with dignitaries and citizens gathering at the Turning Basin to witness the official opening of the Port of Houston, America's newest deep-water port.

C.G. Pillot

Jesse H. Jones

John T. Scott

R. M. Farrar

HOUSTON HARBOR BOARD ON NOVEMBER 10, 1914

Four of Houston's most distinguished citizens made up this body when the Port formally was opened.

Houston Ship Channel and Foot of Main Street, Houston, Texas.

WM. D. CLEVELAND & SONS
WHOLESALE GROCERS. COTTON FACTORS

JASMINE

Channel traffic celebration at the foot of Main Street deemed the "Masterpiece of Congestion."

100

1914

Rotary Club founded

The *Dorothy* arrives at Port with cargo of coal

1914

Sam Houston Area Council of the Boy Scouts established

1914

The Port is christened with "Deep-Water Jubilee"

NOVEMBER 20, 1914

The Port of Houston is officially open! Mayor Ben Campbell officiated the "christening" of the Port of Houston on November 20, 1914. Campbell's daughter, Sue, sprinkled white roses onto the Houston Ship Channel waters with these words, "I christen thee Port of Houston; hither the boats of all nations may come and receive hearty welcome." From the White House, President Woodrow Wilson pressed a button that remotely fired a cannon to commemorate the event.

WORLD WAR I
ABROAD AND AT HOME

The Houston Ship Channel was open and the great vision realized in 1914. That same year saw the completion of American efforts to carve out the Panama Canal, finally connecting the Atlantic and Pacific Oceans, and the United States Navy launch of the *USS Texas*, which would compile a long list of firsts to its credit, including launching a plane from its deck and deploying radar. There was much to celebrate when Woodrow Wilson pushed the button that fired off the ceremonial cannon at Houston's christening of the channel. Yet, that was actually a portent of events that were already beginning to engulf Europe in the summer of 1914.

At that time, the map of Europe was quite different. France, Italy, Great Britain, and Spain were within their familiar borders, but a weighty Austro-Hungarian Empire situated in the center of Europe was surrounded by a much larger Germany and the pre-Soviet tsarist Russian empire, as well as the Ottoman Empire retreating from Europe to what is now Turkey. All of these nations and empires had negotiated alliances, treaties, pacts, and promises but these failed to keep the European continent at peace. The Great War erupted before the channel was complete.

Houstonians, like most of their fellow Americans, initially maintained an isolationist point of view when it came to the war in Europe. Indeed, the "hearty welcome to ships of all nations" ceremonially spoken by young Sue Campbell at the deep-water christening was not to be immediately fulfilled.

USS Texas *(BB-35), battleship of the United States commonly referred to as "Battleship Texas," passes through the Panama Canal.*

THE *USS TEXAS* - 1914

Upon her commissioning in 1914, the **USS Texas** *was sent to Mexican waters by President Wilson to stabilize the "Tampico Incident." The "Battleship Texas" later made numerous sorties into the North Sea during World War I.*

The U.S. Army established Camp Logan in Houston during World War I as a training facility for soldiers prior to deployment in Europe. Its first soldiers were from a base in New Mexico—they were an all-black unit. Unfortunately, a tragic clash between a few of the soldiers and a local sheriff resulted in their march up Washington Boulevard, followed by a riot. The travesty was that the sheriff went unpunished while some soldiers were court-martialed and executed. Camp Logan is now Memorial Park.

1915

RMS Lusitania sunk by
German U-boat

1916

Houston pilots appointed by
governor

1917

United States enters
World War I

Once the channel was deepened and the Port of Houston received larger ocean-going vessels, Houston welcomed sailors from countries like Britain. From the decks of the HMS Durban, *these British Tars (Jack Tar or Tar was a common English term originally used to refer to seamen of the Merchant or Royal Navy) were dreaming of possibilities for shore leave on the streets of Houston.*

1917
Camp Logan and Ellington Field built

1918
Armistice declared

100

As the war began raging across Europe, an early casualty was the cotton trade. Cotton remained the top product transported up and down the channel in 1914; however, wartime restrictions against exports to Europe in 1915 caused a very sharp decline in trade and revenue for the port. Furthermore, proverbial shots were fired at the new Houston Ship Channel from domestic ship owners and shipmasters. Their main concerns were centered on a distrust of the touted channel depth, as well as a general lack of adequate facilities at the docks.

Responding to these potential snags, local citizens banded together without hesitation. They put up their own money for bonds against any damages a ship might suffer if the channel claims proved false. Reading like a *Who's Who* of the day, some of the city notables willing to "put up or shut up" included R. H. and Burke Baker, Joseph Carroll, C. L. Desel, Alexander Cleveland, D. D. Peden, Horace Rice, and H. C. Schumacher. Scores of other Houstonians also pledged their money. With bonds in hand, Houston approached reluctant shipmasters and the owners of shipping lines. Slowly, ships began to come up the channel—first from Philadelphia and then from Central America. Impressed at the confidence of Houstonians, the Southern Steamship Company refused the bond and scheduled

its first vessel to call upon the new deep-water port. That milestone was reached in August of 1915, but not without some prerequisite difficulty.

A storm that month ransacked the Texas Gulf Coast. Loss of life, extensive flooding, and significant damage to property were left in its wake. Against predictions, however, a pleasant surprise was that the channel did not fill in from the storm surge and the swirling, wind-blown currents. As a result, the *Satilla* reached the Turning Basin after only a three-day delay. The *Satilla* was bigger than any previous ship steaming up the channel. Her keel was 312 feet long, and the vessel drew 22 feet of water (the channel's full depth was 25 feet). This ushered in the era of oceangoing vessels coming to Houston. In those first years, profitability for the Port and the lines serving it was elusive—especially during World War I, into which America was about to be drawn.

> *"The arrival of the* Satilla *is the culmination of all our hopes and years of dreams."*
> —HOUSTON MAYOR BEN CAMPBELL

The Satilla, *carrying 1,925 tons of general cargo, was the first deep-water steamer to arrive in Houston after the inauguration of the Port of Houston and its Ship Channel. She arrived on August 22, 1915, following a severe storm that rocked the upper Texas Gulf Coast and facilities in Galveston Bay. The Port of Houston withstood nature's thrashing and received the* Satilla. *This started an era of constant runs by deep-water vessels between Houston and other American ports.*

1918
30 industrial facilities line banks of Buffalo Bayou

WAR AND PEACE, BOOM AND CRASH

By April 1917 the United States declared war, and within months, thousands of American servicemen were on their way across the Atlantic. Also deployed was a U.S. Navy battleship group, with which the *USS Texas* was supposed to sail. Minor damage in an exercise delayed her departure but ultimately she was able to serve with Britain's Grand Fleet during the war. America didn't have to endure the war for long—only 18 months. In that time frame, the city of Houston committed 15,000 of her bravest sons to uniform. Of those, nearly 150 gave the ultimate sacrifice. At home, virtually every civic organization in the city mobilized to sell Liberty Bonds and to collect surgical and other needed supplies. One such club was the War Mothers Association, which grew from 58 charter members to 300 by war's end. An armistice was signed on November 11, 1918, and Houstonians took to the streets of downtown for a victory sing.

Benjamin C. Allin

Benjamin C. Allin III, an engineer and World War I Army officer, became the first director of the Port of Houston (1919–1931). He restored organization to World War I condemned overstock in tattered warehouses, and built wharves and warehouses under the authority given to him by the newly formed Board of Navigation and Canal Commissioners. He continued the development of cotton export, building on Houston's position as the largest spot market in the world. The Houston Port Bureau was formed in 1929 out of his conviction that the Port would require constant promotion due to its inland location. Fortunately, Port leadership did not buy into the old saying, "Once built, it would be used and run itself."

In 1929, Benjamin Allin developed and patented an industrial site and railway access design that ports and maritime industries used for many years. His warehouse and wharf shed design features a spur of the main railway line running through it so that rail cars could be loaded and unloaded without delaying traffic on the mainline.

J. Russell Wait followed Allin as Port director (1931–1947) leading the Port through the daunting depression years and World War II. The most significant events during his tenure as director were the purchase of all city-owned port facilities by the Port and the approval of two tunnels to replace ferry boats which had slowed navigation for deep-water vessels.

This typical cotton warehouse was jammed to the brim in 1919 with a portion of the 45,400 bales exported. The number jumped to almost 1.3 million bales in 1924.

Cotton flatcars stand in rows at the Houston Union Station railroad.

100

PEACETIME GROWTH

While peacetime settled over much of the world, an explosion of development ignited from the Port. Knowing that Washington, D.C. was about to appropriate funds to help improve American ports, including the Port of Houston, Ross Sterling began a plan to upgrade facilities and facilitate long-term growth. Sterling was one of the founders of the Humble Oil Company, and his star had risen in Texas since 1911. In fact, he had already been associated with the port for a few years. Like Jesse Jones, Sterling had a vision for the port and the resources to make it happen. His influential position as publisher of the "Houston Post-Dispatch" allowed him a means to align public opinion with that vision.

Obvious to Sterling, and probably everyone else, was that cotton and oil would lead the way for growth. A viable ship channel of proven depth suddenly made the lowly regarded bayou a prime location for manufacturing. The cotton trade already knew this, and it wasn't long before Houston took full advantage of that knowledge. A symbolic kick-off event for cotton took place in November of 1919. It was then that the *Merry Mount* pulled up dockside at the Turning Basin. She was loaded with almost 21,000 bales of cotton, sent steaming down the Houston Ship Channel into the Gulf, and ultimately across the Atlantic for direct delivery to Europe with no stops in New Orleans.

The Houston downtown building boom of 1927, which was unequaled until the first years of the 1960s; in various stages of their "sky scratcher" construction are the Niels Esperson Building, the Lamar Hotel (lower left corner), the Gulf Building (population approximately 292,350).

THE *MERRY MOUNT*

100

The opening of the Port of Houston as a deep-water port and the dredging of the Houston Ship Channel allowed ocean-worthy steam freighters to sail directly to Europe from Houston. The first vessel to do so was the S.S. Merry Mount, which took on a load of cotton valued at 1 million dollars bound for Liverpool.

Loading nearly 21,000 bales of cotton onto the Merry Mount, *the largest shipment from the U.S. Gulf for several years.*

1918
First refinery built on Houston Ship Channel

1919
S.S. Merry Mount, first ship bound for Europe, leaves the Port

The Long Reach wharf was the first of its kind at the Port of Houston, built for cotton magnate, Anderson, Clayton and Company, and spurred on by the booming cotton industry. Today this location is in the hub of the Turning Basin Terminal. Anderson, Clayton and Company became the world's largest cotton brokerage firm. In 1916, Frank Anderson, Monroe D. Anderson (better known as MD Anderson), and William Clayton moved their national headquarters from Oklahoma to Houston.

LONG REACH DOCKS' GRASP
EXTENDS TO PRESENT TURNING BASIN

1920

Port of Houston becomes 6th largest in U.S.

1921

Cotton annual transports almost 500,000 bales

1922

Upgrades to public docks and Long Reach docks begin

Unification of City Harbor Board and Harris County Houston Ship Channel Navigation District

LONGREACH ANDERSON-CLAYTON WHARF
THIS 1700 FEET LONG STRUCTURE
COMPLETED IN RECORD TIME OF 90 DAYS
ERECTED 1923

Labor force viewing concrete piling used for Long Reach construction in 1923. Some say Long Reach derived its name from being the longest and straightest stretch of the shoreline in the upper bayou. Others believe the name came from the fact that these docks took quite a "spell" to travel round trip, from the original downtown docks at the foot of Main Street.

AMERICA'S INDUSTRIAL FRONTIER

Earliest shipping activity at Long Reach (presently part of Turning Basin Terminal) proving that the Ship Channel was ready to be the "Gateway to Commerce" in the Gulf Coast and beyond.

1923

Pilots under the control of the Port

1924

Port Terminal Railroad organized

EASING A CORNER: Manchester Terminal at top center and Sinclair Refinery tanker berths. The new channel on the right was cut 1912 to 1914 to remove the sharp bend, and in 1966 the entire point was dredged to make a second turning basin.

Almost instantly, as part of Sterling's long-term plan, upgrades began on facilities along the channel, including the Long Reach Wharf by Anderson, Clayton and Company for its subsidiary, the Houston Compress Company. In fact, throughout the 1920s, work was almost frantic to keep up with continually increasing channel traffic. Cotton transports alone went from less than half a million bales in 1921 to just under 2 million by year-end 1929. The city of Houston completed a series of upgrades that included six new wharves and significant improvements to existing ones, as well as additional railway capacity. But the improvements to and expansion of port facilities were not solely driven by cotton. During that same decade, grain tonnage went from zero tons in 1919 to 4.9 million in 1930. A public grain elevator had been built in 1926 and later expanded to meet demand.

Industry, too, saw an ideal position for both bringing in raw materials and shipping out products. As early as 1918, there were over three dozen separate industrial facilities lining the banks of the channel above and below the Turning Basin. This number grew as Houston experienced a significant shift in its commerce from a spot market or distribution center to a manufacturing center.

Flour and coffee joined kingpins cotton and oil as major exports from the Port of Houston.

1924
Memorial Park opens

The American Maid Flour Mill & Grain Elevator facilities were built in 1922 for the manufacture of high grade flour for domestic use and export.

AUTO INDUSTRY LIFTS EXPORTS

Roadsters at the Port are lifted for their next passage. In 1920, the Port of Houston was ranked sixth largest port in U.S., just six years after its inauguration as a deep-water port.

The roll-on/roll-off (RO-RO) of automobiles directly from ships is widely utilized at Houston Ship Channel terminals.

Built in 1921, this Ford Assembly Plant operated in Houston for nearly 20 years before it became a factory for aircraft parts during World War II. In 1946 it was sold to Maxwell House, a division of General Foods (see next page).

1925

Port launches its first fireboat, *Port Houston*

Maxwell House advertising coffee, a major Port product for 100 years.

STRONG COFFEE INDUSTRY

Coffee bags being unloaded to portable conveyors on a Port wharf in 1922.

In the early days, cotton was king at the Port of Houston. But today there is a new bumper crop crossing the docks—green coffee beans. Import cargo to the Houston Ship Channel arrives from a diverse list of countries including Mexico, Russia, Italy, Angola, China, Egypt and Romania. The Port became the fourth designated Green Coffee Port in 2003 by the New York Board of Trade (NYBOT).

At the end of 2006, Maximus Coffee Group successfully completed the acquisition of the historic Maxwell House coffee plant located in Houston's East End. This purchase saved over 350 jobs and ensures that Houston will remain an international coffee center many years into the future.

1926
Public Grain Elevator is built at Turning Basin

LET THERE BE LIGHTS

After the war, lighting paved the way for further development. Many shipping lines had long prohibited their vessels from night navigation through parts of the channel because it had few or no lights. Originally, the channel was marked by 11 lights, tended by members of the U.S. Lighthouse Service who would light each oil lamp by hand from a rowboat. In 1933, a series of 32 acetylene channel lights were placed between Lynchburg and the Sinclair Refinery, permitting 24-hour use of the waterway. Night navigation increased dramatically from 110 ships in 1930 to 943 ships in 1936. That helped the next year's Port figures improve to 2,732 ship arrivals with a combined ship and barge freight of 23,800,415 tons.

Today the Port works around the clock with energy efficient lighting and control systems.

Labor-intensive methods to lay pipe the "old fashioned way" in 1925 from the South Texas fields to Houston, by the Houston Pipe Line Company.

UNDERWATER AND UNDERGROUND PIPELINES BURIED

This Shell pipeline crossing in 1931 connected facilities on both sides of the Port. Further lowering and/or replacing of pipelines became necessary as deepening of channel has been an ongoing endeavor.

BIRTH OF THE PETROCHEMICAL INDUSTRY

Sinclair built the first refinery along 700 acres of the Houston Ship Channel in 1918 to process "black gold." Legend says Santa Anna buried golden treasure under this same site while camped there during his march to defeat at San Jacinto Battleground, 10 miles away.

Baytown *was the first oil tanker at the 1919 Humble Refinery.*

BLACK GOLD, TEXAS TEA

Along with the cotton, grain, and industrial contributers to channel traffic, the real giant was emerging. Refiners had taken quick advantage of the Port's open land, fresh water, and close proximity to producing fields. First on the scene were the Petroleum Refining Company in 1918 and the Sinclair Oil Company. Humble Oil secured 1,500 acres for itself, too. A decade later there were no less than eight refineries with a combined refining capacity of 3,250,000 barrels per month. By 1930 there were some 27 tanker lines operating in the Port, and in that same year almost 4 million tons of petroleum products were transported.

S/S Winifred *with first cargo of crude from the oil fields of Tampico, Mexico in 1915, greeted by a motorized sailing yacht.*

1928

Port introduces *RJ Cummins*, its first inspection boat

Goose Creek Oil Field reached maximum production in 1918 and became the location of the first offshore wells in Texas, and the second group of offshore wells in the United States. The field remains active, having produced over 150 million barrels of oil in its 100-year history.

With the discovery of the Goose Creek Oil Field in 1907, the rival communities of Goose Creek, Pelly, and East Baytown developed as early boomtowns. They later consolidated in 1948 and agreed upon the name of Baytown as their new city. Between 1912 and 1925 the Goose Creek Oil Field was the 4th largest oil producer in Texas. Humble Oil and Refining Company developed this field in 1916 which led to the building of Baytown Refinery, one of their largest refineries in the world.

Humble Refinery, Baytown

1929
Wall Street crashes and
the Great Depression begins

100

With World War I came both the widespread introduction of the automobile and airplane. Demands for fuel and lubricants brought a vast array of industrial developments to the Ship Channel. Oil refineries and terminals began to handle huge amounts of crude and refined oils through pipelines and tankers.

Shell's Houston Refinery (pictured beside the channel) was one of the first to locate on the Houston Ship Channel and went onstream in 1929, followed by Shell Chemical Corporation (to the far right). Their first units were operational before Pearl Harbor in 1941.

This plant, Texas Petrochemicals Houston, is one of the major petrochemical plants along the Houston Ship Channel. Like others on or near the Port, the development of these facilities was fueled by the desperate need for synthetic rubber during World War II since Japan controlled rubber in Asia. Goodyear was built on the Port and became a major producer of styrene and butadiene used to produce synthetic rubber. Jesse H. Jones was influential in the U.S. funding for research of synthetic rubber which became reality in 1943—at a critical point in the war.

Houston Fuel Oil Terminal sitting on a 312-acre footprint at one of the widest parts of the Houston Ship Channel, serves as one of the largest trading centers for residual fuel oil and crude oil in the world. Its 13.8 million barrel storage terminal also establishes this terminal as the largest provider of residual fuel oil in the U.S. Gulf Coast. The San Jacinto Monument rises in the background.

The petrochemical facilities and oil refineries along the Houston Ship Channel never sleep. The Houston Ship Channel is home to the largest petrochemical complex in the U.S.

1929
Cotton annual transports 2 million bales

USS HOUSTON COMES TO CALL

For an inland port that attracted little attention, Houston's little ditch was doing a watershed of business. To celebrate a decade of unbridled growth, the latest cruiser of the United States Navy visited the Port of Houston. Her name was the *USS Houston*—a name conferred upon the vessel after some considerable petition writing (and lobbying) by the populace and notables of her namesake. In 1929, she was ceremoniously christened with a bottle of Buffalo Bayou water in Newport News, Virginia by Elizabeth Holcombe, the young daughter of Houston's long-time mayor, Oscar Holcombe. An overall length of 600 feet, 570 feet at the keel, made her the largest floating vessel to have entered the channel as of 1930.

Arrival of U.S. Cruiser Houston *in 1930 draws 200,000 visitors. In 1931, she became the flagship of the Asiatic Fleet, and three years later would serve twice as "Navy One"—carrying President Franklin D. Roosevelt on inspection cruises to various U.S. ports.*

"OLD IRONSIDES" VISITS

USS Constitution passes the Reserve Power Plant of the Houston Lighting & Power Company (HL&P).

Built in 1797 and achieving fame in the War of 1812, USS Constitution, "Old Ironsides," visits the port in 1932. Assurances were made and repeated that the 188 foot masts would pass safely under the power lines near Baytown. Nervous officials were greatly relieved when they watched it sail past with a slim 3-foot clearance overhead. Perhaps it was the only ship to visit the Port of Houston in the 1930s that paused because of the height rather than the depth of channel.

THE GREAT DEPRESSION

Ironically, as Houstonians were celebrating the glorious economics of the Roaring Twenties, the Great Depression was spreading across the planet, raining a deluge of ruin that still influences governments' decision-making. For Houston, the Crash of '29 was like the shudder initially felt by the Titanic when she struck an iceberg. It took time, but the city finally felt the sinking effects. For the first few years of the 1930s, tonnage levels dropped below what they were in 1929. Intervals between ships steaming up the channel grew longer and longer—to the point where the ranks of longshoreman withered to skeleton crews. Adding to the issue was the fact that the port had become a conflagration that not only included city, county, state, and federal bureaucracies, but private ones as well. There were hosts of labor issues, financing challenges, maintenance obstacles, and operations difficulties.

Things were tough, but Houstonians tried to remain optimistic. Much faith was placed with Jesse Jones, whose efforts had averted the collapse of several Houston banks. His leadership became legendary and the U.S. Government tapped him for the board of the Reconstruction Finance Corporation (RFC). President Roosevelt eventually appointed Jones as chairman. In the meantime, Houston was by no means unscathed in the crisis.

Whole families struggled to earn pennies a day to pay for food, if available. This was also the time of the Dust Bowl, when much of America's farming heartland became more like the Sahara Desert than amber waves of grain. Indeed, the once proud Public Grain Elevator at the Port had handled 2,967,981 bushels in 1932, but it was largely empty between 1933 and 1935. Houston grain exports did not resume until 1938.

Longshoremen guide cotton bales into the "hold" of a ship for export. Cotton remained a labor intensive cargo product up to the mid-twentieth century.

The Houston Public Grain Elevator was built in 1926. It was designed for 1 million bushel capacity, expanded to triple capacity four years later, and eventually built out to 6 million bushel capacity.

Ships were made of wood and men were made of steel in 1922 when the longshoremen were loading the S.S. Sula *at the Port of Houston.*

1930

Grain tonnage reaches 5 million bushels

1930

Refining capacity reaches
3.25 million barrels/month

1930

Twenty-seven oil tankers service
refineries at the Port

COMMISSIONERS
D. BARKER,
ALLIE ANDERSON,

OSCAR HOLCOMBE,
MAYOR

COMMISSIONERS
S. A. STARKEY,
JAS. H. B. HOUSE,

City of Houston
Texas

H. A. GILES,
CITY CONTROLLER

STERLING HOGAN,
CITY SECRETARY

"THE EVER CHANGING SKYLINE"

A CITY CELEBRATES ITS TITLE "BRIGHT SPOT OF THE NATION"

Hardship seemed to be a recurring challenge for Houston and her port. Still, men worked hard to keep trade alive in some fashion and to preserve traffic in the channel. The refining industry became a significant lifeline for the Houston Ship Channel since machines and vehicles needed fuel to operate, and the country still needed petroleum products for various industrial uses. In fact, Houston was declared the oil refining capital of the world during the 1930s, with much of the tonnage traveling up and down the channel made up of petroleum and chemical products. Combined with other efforts, the port tonnage continued to increase. In 1934 ship arrivals at the Port reached 2,489, and the combined barge and shipping freight was 19,292,629 tons.

"The Channel of Houston" float, 1930

1930
USS Houston visits Port of Houston

1932
Port handles 2.97 million bushels of grain

Downtown Houston and the "World's Largest Cotton Port" float, 1930.

"...stronger than oceans, wind-swept, God-blessed, and teeming with people of all kinds living in harmony and peace, a city with free ports that hummed with commerce and creativity, and if there had to be city walls, the walls had doors and the doors were open to anyone with the will and the heart to get here."

—JOHN WINTHROP

"The Gateway to the World" Houston Chamber of Commerce float, 1930

1932

Jesse H. Jones becomes chairman of Reconstruction Finance Corp

A longshoreman, whose brawn is part of the strength of the Port, keeps a keen eye on cargo.

A feminine touch tops the cotton cargo.

1933

Lights installed along Houston Ship Channel allowing night navigation

1934

University of Houston became a four-year institution

Ship arrivals reach 2,500 carrying 19.3 million tons of cargo

1934

Houston becomes oil refining capital of the world

Houston 1939 downtown aerial photo (population approximately 384,500). Only 100 years old as a city, feeling its way out of the Great Depression, and home to the fastest growing port in the country, Houston was becoming the petrochemical capital of the world with 37% of the total U.S. refining capacity. Fortune magazine summarized, "From the way things are going, Houston's future seems limitless. Along the banks of the Houston Ship Channel is the world's greatest concentration of new-built industry. Here might a modern Horace Greeley counsel the youth to 'Go Southwest, young man.'"

100

FDR VISITS THE HOUSTON SHIP CHANNEL

Jesse H. Jones, far left, President Roosevelt, middle, and group on rear platform of Presidential Special Train arriving in Houston, 1936.

With a bit of sunshine peeking though the cloudy Depression Era, Houstonians took time to celebrate their state's centennial in 1935. Citizens turned out at the San Jacinto Battleground to commemorate the birth of Texas. Dignitaries of all sorts attended and delivered speeches. Franklin Roosevelt had been on hand, after having toured the Houston Ship Channel on a private yacht and the Port facilities in a car with his RFC Chairman, Jesse Jones. In his address, Roosevelt gave an endorsement to the importance of the city of Houston and its ship channel:

"THIS AND THE EASTERN PART OF YOUR GREAT STATE, THROUGH WHICH I CAME THIS MORNING, CAN TRULY BE CALLED THE CRADLE OF TEXAS LIBERTY. I HAVE BEEN GLAD TO REVISIT YOUR BEAUTIFUL CITY OF HOUSTON. TYPICAL OF AMERICAN ENTERPRISE, YOU HAVE BROUGHT THE COMMERCE OF THE WORLD TO YOUR DOOR BY THE SHIP CANAL THROUGH WHICH I HAVE RECENTLY PASSED."

Aboard the Captiva II *yacht, President Roosevelt and other dignitaries enjoyed an inspection cruise of the Port of Houston, 1936.*

100

President Roosevelt tours the upper level of the Port by open car. While addressing the public, he reiterated the Port's value and importance to U.S. commerce.

1934

Intracoastal Canal System links Houston with
the Mississippi River system of navigation

1935

Depression relief for Houstonians
reaches more than $8 million

1936

Texas and Houston celebrate Centennials

FDR tours Port of Houston, declares it "vital"

THE SAN JACINTO MONUMENT

USS Texas *battleship celebrates its centennial in 2014. After service in World War I and World War II, the San Jacinto Battleground became its permanent location in 1948.*

In some ways the centennial celebration may have served to signal the new birth for the city. The Port of Houston was about to be recognized as fourth among the nation's ocean ports. An increase in ship arrivals totaled 3,077 with a combined ship and barge freight of 26,737,394 tons. These figures would contribute to Houston's ranking as the number one port in the South. By the close of the 1930s, tonnage neared 30 million. Cargo was made up of paper goods, resumed grain exports, coffee imports, and automobile imports and exports. As always, Houston pulled itself up by its bootstraps and endured—pushing forward to find success.

1936

Houston Port & Traffic Bureau established

Freight reaches 26.7 million tons

USS TEXAS 1914 – 2014 Centennial

USS Texas battleship and the San Jacinto Monument. The Texas battleship was built in 1914 during the height of the Dreadnought Era, when it is said that battleships were at the pinnacle of their influence. This is the last Dreadnought Era battleship still afloat in the world. While earning five Battle Stars in World War II, the Texas had a notable number of firsts including the first battleship to launch aircraft by catapult, accommodate a permanently assigned contingent of Marines, and house anti-aircraft guns, in addition to the being the first battleship to become both a permanent Museum Ship and National Historic Landmark.

1936

Port of Houston ranked first in the South

1937

Freight tonnage reaches 30 million

Port of Houston ranked second behind NY in tonnage

SHARED CENTENNIALS

A majestic view of the canal on the "passageway between the seas."

Present day expansion of Panama Canal Locks to open in 2016 at cost of 5.2 billion dollars.

PANAMA CANAL, "THE BIG DIG" 1914 - 2014

The Port of Houston and the Panama Canal share completion dates, centennials, and both span 50-plus miles. The Panama Canal is located 1,550 miles from Houston, the closest major U.S. Gulf port. Author Marilyn Sibley wrote regarding the closely related work of the channel and the canal, "The men working on the Houston Ship Channel read monthly reports from the Canal Zone with interest and were sometimes pleased to learn that they had excavated more dirt during a certain length of time than workers at the Isthmus."

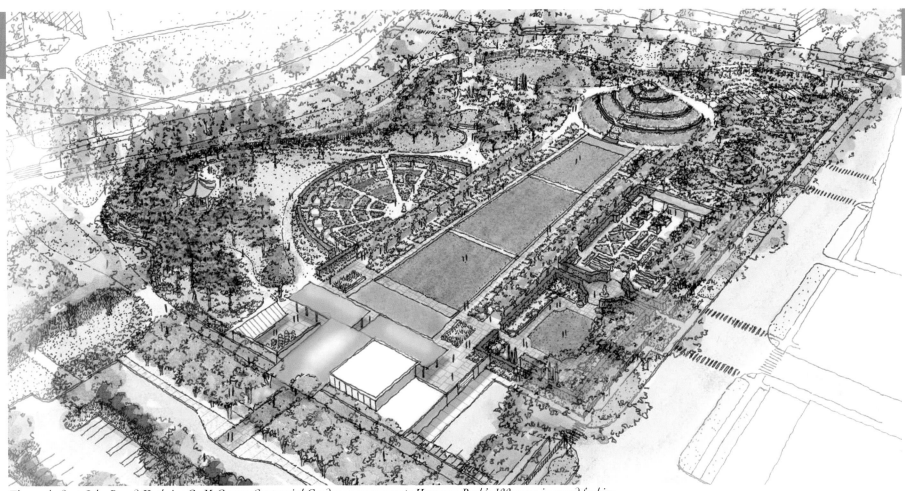

The resplendent John P. and Kathrine G. McGovern Centennial Gardens commemorate Hermann Park's 100 years in grand fashion.

HERMANN PARK 1914 - 2014

Hermann Park was presented to the City of Houston in 1914 by George Hermann. The 445-acre park is located next to the Texas Medical Center and home to the Houston Zoo, Miller Outdoor Theater, Houston Museum of Natural Science, Houston Garden Center, Hermann Park Golf Course, and future Centennial Park. Hermann Park hosts 6 million visitors per year.

THEN

An early performance at Miller Outdoor Theater, built in 1923.

NOW

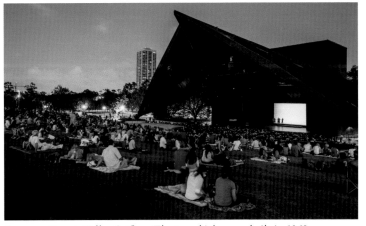

Lawn seating at Miller Outdoor Theater which was rebuilt in 1969.

The Sam Houston Monument is located in front of Hermann Park and depicts General Sam Houston on horseback leading his men into the battle of San Jacinto. The monument is positioned to point towards the battleground.

During the closing years of the 1930s, a new component to port tonnage was the export of scrap metal. Mountains of it lined portions of the channel. The piles were made up of old cars, appliances, furniture frames, cushion springs, and just about anything metal and salvageable. Between 1937 and 1939, the lion's share of scrap metal was innocently bound for one spot in the Pacific—Imperial Japan.

1937

Houston Municipal Airport, which would later become William P. Hobby Airport, is opened

1937

Port Houston exports scrap metal to Japan

1937

Japan invades China

WAR AND RECOVERY

Political upheavals, bread lines, huge unemployment, the Dust Bowl, agrarian collapse, and a continuing rise of organized crime were symbolic of a dark period following the Crash of '29. Houston suffered, too, as did its port. The people had it tough, but a turnaround began in 1936. The Great Depression was more of a hiccup in terms of revenues and tonnage for the port. It never totally ceased operations, nor did it fall into neglect. Between 1930 and 1939, the channel was deepened and widened twice to accommodate the ever-increasing size of blue-water vessels—sparse as their visits sometimes were. Nevertheless, by 1940 the channel depth was almost 35 feet and widened to over 400 feet in Galveston Bay (the width dropped to 300 feet at Morgan's Cut). In addition, navigation lights and beacons were installed to enable night traffic through the channel.

SELLING WAR BONDS: Will Clayton of Anderson, Clayton and Company, Mrs. Clayton, Mrs. Jones and Jesse Jones

The M10 tank destroyers and DUKW (nicknamed "Ducks") were loaded at the Port of Houston for shipment to World War II campaigns in Africa and Sicily. The awkward looking "Ducks" were amphibious jeeps with a propeller and six wheels to climb out onto beaches and riverbanks, demonstrating another example of American ingenuity.

Brown shipbuilding yard produced wartime ships.

Women pitched in from start to finish.

Floods over the decade brought to light the need for controls, not only for the benefit of upland areas but to handle gutter wash and dumping into the bayou, which contributed to shoaling in the Turning Basin and other spots downstream, and impeding maintenance dredging. Environmental awareness emerged and eventually flood control plans were developed to help curb some of these problems.

Part of America's recovery, and in particular Houston's, was marked by improvements in trade and shipping. Jobs were coming back to the area and attracting workers and their families. By 1940, Houston's population swelled to 384,514, making it the 21st largest city in the United States. But while the population was growing, ship arrivals fell, yet freight tonnage was almost the same as it was in 1939. The fact that five steamship lines stopped their service to Houston and many other ports was a sign of storm clouds on the horizon.

In the opening months of America's participation in World War II, almost all commercial shipping halted. Pouring salt on that wound was the wartime gathering of men and material that was concentrated on the East and West Coasts, which were logical and natural departure points for convoys heading across their respective oceans. But this left the ports along the Gulf of Mexico high and dry—at first. From a revenue standpoint, that was a low point, but it may have saved lives. Few Americans are aware of just how dangerous the Gulf of Mexico was by the summer of 1942. Earlier that year, night skies often lit up with explosions along the Atlantic coast as German U-boats picked off freighters, targeting their silhouettes against the bright skylines of coastal cities. Once the United States caught on and shifted tactics to restrict night navigation and to assign escorts to freighters and convoys, the Eastern Seaboard hunting grounds of the U-boats dried up. Undeterred, they went stalking in the Gulf of Mexico.

U-boat warfare inflicted numerous American losses and in one month alone, U-boats sank 56 merchant vessels. Germany also entered into a secret agreement with Mexico for fuel, and it was speculated that U-boats were being refueled at Mexican ports on the Gulf. It was also speculated that at least a few espionage agents were put ashore at some of Texas' more remote coastlines. Records are scant, but there were very deep incursions into U.S. coastal waters by German U-boats.

While the war dammed up shipping out to the Gulf, other activity at the Port of Houston continued. Re-entering the port "scene" at this point is Jesse H. Jones. In 1940, Jones was tapped by President Roosevelt to serve as Secretary of Commerce. It is worth noting that Jones was a Republican serving in a Democratic administration. Jones had proven repeatedly that he was an economic leader. Benefiting from that leadership, time and again, was the Port of Houston. During World War II, he made sure industrial growth was heaped upon the channel.

The first to receive phone calls from Jones were the oil companies. The engine of modern warfare is the internal combustion engine. Not only did the refineries along the channel shift into high gear to meet wartime production needs, they also expanded. Aircraft, tanks, jeeps, and ships immediately needed fuel, and munitions factories needed toluene for trinitrotoluene — TNT.

1944 depiction of Houston Ship Channel security watches for enemy intrusions at night on the cover of a Port publication.

A crowd watches the launching a sub-chaser at Seabrook Yacht Corporation, 1940.

1939
San Jacinto Battleground Monument opens to public

1939
Germany launches Blitzkrieg

1939
Freight tonnage reaches 30 million

SHIPS AND STEEL ASSIST THE WAR EFFORT

In 1942, Sheffield Steel built a $17 million plant on a 600-acre tract fronting the ship channel, which instantly became Houston's largest industrial plant.

Also at the behest of Jesse Jones, the petroleum industry helped solve a basic military need. Japan's early command in the Pacific meant that rubber was under its control. America needed either other sources of rubber or had to figure out how to synthesize it. In addition to paper drives and scrap metal drives, there were rubber drives. For much of the war, American drivers rode on bald tires and patched up holes in tubes as best they could. Many companies, like the milk industry, reverted to horse-drawn carriages to service their routes. Conservation and recycling old tires weren't enough. In 1942, a good synthetic rubber was developed, and its formula included a petroleum by-product. Jones recognized the abilities of his neighbors along the Houston Ship Channel, the "can do" attitude of the workforce, and the advantages of the channel's close proximity to oil supplies, existing shipping, and rail facilities. Jones made sure that two of the plants were located near Houston.

Houston's deep-water port and its protected location from open waters made it an ideal location for other defense facilities. The U.S. Army established an ordinance depot, and close by was Hughes Tool Company's Dickson Gun Plant.

World War II gave birth to two shipbuilding operations on the channel during the war. The first was a subsidiary of New York's Todd Shipbuilding Corporation—the Houston Shipbuilding Corporation. The other was the Brown Shipbuilding Company. Together, they churned out over 572 vessels for the United States that included Liberty Ships, sub chasers, landing craft, and destroyers. Before the first hull was launched, however, Houston would suffer a blow to her morale.

1940

City of Houston population at 384,500

Brown Shipbuilding Company pioneered the broadside launching and produced more than 300 vessels by the end of the war.

Liberty Ships turned out by Todd Shipyards helped to defeat infamous German U-boats efforts to starve out the British.

1940
Houston dismantled the last of its streetcar system

Jesse Jones becomes Secretary of Commerce

1941
Japan attacks United States at Pearl Harbor

The *USS Houston* steamed into the Port of Houston pay tribute as the cities' namesake back in 1930, but she was still close to the hearts of Houstonians. Just two months after Pearl Harbor, early in 1942, the *Houston* and the Australian cruiser *Perth* were inadvertently caught in a trap while taking on superior enemy forces. They sank one transport and forced three others to beach before meeting their fate. *Perth* succumbed to enemy fire first, leaving the *Houston* to fight alone for another hour until she sank to the bottom of the Coral Sea. Of the original crew of 1,061 men, 368 survived. On May 30, 1942, 1,000 new Navy recruits, known as the Houston Volunteers, were sworn in at a dedication ceremony in downtown Houston to replace those believed lost on *USS Houston* (CL-81).

USS Houston *passes the Battleground.*

In 1942, after receiving word that the USS Houston *had been sunk, hundreds of Houstonians were sworn in to replace the men lost and to avenge the fallen cruiser.*

PEACE AND PROGRESS

100

Established by the Army Air Service on May 21, 1917, Ellington Field was one of the initial World War I Army Air Service installations when aviation was in its infancy. Originally created as a training facility, Ellington Airport is currently used by military, commercial, NASA aircraft, and general aviation sectors. Ellington Airport is one of the few airfields built for World War I training purposes still in operation today. The above photo shows its expanded layout during World War II.

Germany surrendered in May 1945 and four months after that, Japan surrendered. As the United States gained control of the seas in early 1945, commercial shipping resumed. Ship arrivals to the Port of Houston quickly climbed, and cargo tonnage started increasing, too. In fact, within a year of the end of the war, cargo handling exceeded the pre-war peak set in 1939 and reached almost 32 million tons.

A lot had changed during World War II, and more change was ahead. During the Depression and then the war, badly needed new construction and upgrades to port facilities had been sidelined. That was not unique to the Port of Houston; other ports needed to make improvements, too. Almost the whole of Eurasia needed to rebuild after the war and in America neglected infrastructure needed to be fixed, expanded, or replaced. All combined, this created high demands for labor and material, causing price hikes everywhere. While money had been secured for many of these efforts, the original amounts appropriated were often not enough to keep pace with post-war inflation. Nevertheless, officials kept at it and made improvements when and where possible.

1942

German U-boats prowl Gulf of Mexico

USS Houston sunk in the Pacific

1943

Wartime industries in full swing along Houston Ship Channel

1943

Synthetic rubber was mass produced for the first time by two new Houston area plants and shipped for use in World War II through the Port of Houston

HOUSTON RANKS AS FIRST IN GULF

The war had its impact on port leadership, too. Officials resigned over the course of that period in order to take war-related positions, departed for military service, or their terms ended. Frequent changes continued in the postwar years, too. Although port leadership shifted, the operational agenda was sustained. Albert Thomas was the local congressman with U.S. House of Representatives. Much of his early focus was on the improvement of the Houston Ship Channel, resulting in a fresh channel survey in 1941. Recommendations to widen parts of the channel were made in 1944, and within a year, money was appropriated thanks to the influence and perseverance of Congressman Thomas. In addition, efforts were completed to acquire the last of the City of Houston harbor facilities. In doing so, the Port Authority now had full control over all onshore public facilities along the channel. They just needed to be improved and maintained. There was also the issue of labor and material.

Somehow, the Port seemed to make do in the early postwar years. While public facilities were slow to be refurbished or expanded, the Houston Ship Channel exploded with industrial traffic. The wartime legacy left Houston and its port with a growing petrochemical complex emerging with new products and processes for world markets. Where possible, defense industries were retooled and converted to output for commercial purposes.

America as a whole became the breadbasket to a hungry, war-weary world. Much of that grain was shipped out through the Port of Houston. Moreover, America was rebuilding Europe, Japan, and the Pacific. With industrial output of the nation in overdrive, between 1946 and 1952, Port of Houston activity grew to more than 3,700 vessels carrying 46.6 million tons. Over that same period, the Port of Houston became the second largest U.S. port in overall tonnage. In 1948, a milestone was reached when the value of the tonnage exceeded a billion dollars, and the value had grown to 2 billion dollars by 1952.

DEEP-WATER SECURITY OVER 52 MILES

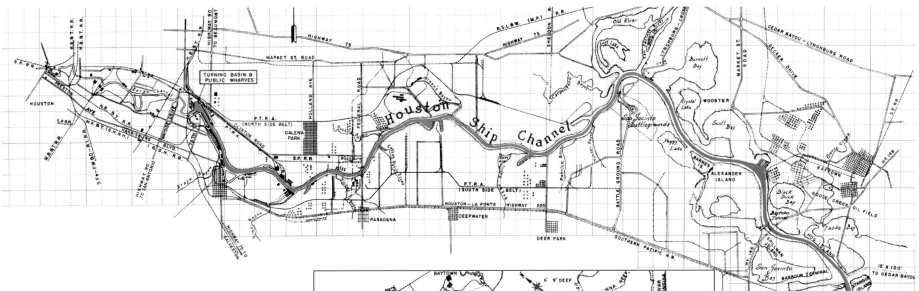

ID CARDS TODAY...

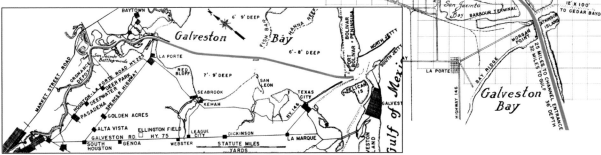

SCHROETER, THOMAS G

Expires 05DEC2012

Transportation Worker Identification Credential

The first Transportation Worker Identification Credential (TWIC) card issued by the U.S. Department of Homeland Security in Houston. Tamper resistant TWIC cards ensure that individuals who pose a threat do not gain access to secure areas of the nation's maritime transportation system. TWIC was instituted in 2008.

AND YESTERDAY

PORT OF HOUSTON AUTHORITY

ID NO. 000012885

PHA - SMALL BUSINESS

GILDA RAMIREZ

EXPIRES: 04/23/2016

Port Security began long before 9/11 as seen in a typical ID card carried by longshoremen during the years of World War II. Multi-generational cards are represented by the Ramirez family with over 70 years of employment at the Port.

1944
Bond approved to build Washburn and Baytown Tunnels

1945
World War II ends with surrender of Germany and Japan

1947
Texas City explosion

POST-WAR COMMERCE

100

High and dry like a beached whale, the tanker Fort Mercer *awaits stern section at Todd Shipyards, Houston, 1953.*

1947

Sam Houston I inspection boat replaces *RJ Cummins*

Houston voters defeat the first-ever referendum for citywide zoning

1948

The Gulf Freeway, Texas' first freeway opens as U.S. Highway 75, signaling the beginning of freeway construction in the city

Logs are lifted for transport to paper mills, 1948.

The pulp business was joined by numerous industries in officially ending the Depression in the Greater Houston Area by building new plants and mills along the Houston Ship Channel in the late 1930s. Once again, commerce leading to Houston's growth and success was re-energized by the resurgent channel.

Today large rolls of paper used in publication of newspapers are regularly shipped from the Port to South America.

A decade after the conclusion of World War II, the Port of Houston hit a wall. Ten years of growth and expansion came to a screeching halt when tonnage numbers flattened out during 1953 and 1954. By 1955 the Port of Houston was down in ranking from being second only to New York to being in fourth place behind New Orleans and Philadelphia. Although there was a mild recession during those years, the reality was that the Port was taken for granted—by both the citizens it served and the Port leadership.

It was in the mid-1950s that port capacity was not only at its limit, but there were no clear plans to improve or expand it. As a result, Houston was turning away business while sitting on its laurels. Concurrently, New Orleans, an old port competitor of Houston, was executing a major expansion. A few new players, like Corpus Christi, had popped up along the Gulf Coast, too. Business had other places to go, and Houston needed to rekindle its once-aggressive thinking to do what was needed to fuel growth, or business was going elsewhere.

Providence again played its hand in Houston's favor when, in 1956, two defining and powerful forces were about to converge on the Port of Houston—containerization and renewed leadership.

A ship is turned around in the Turning Basin by a tugboat in 1959.

General cargo gains as new facilities are completed in 1959. Port of Houston ranks as second in the U.S.

From far left: Rice Stadium, the Shamrock Hotel, Texas Medical Center, and downtown Houston in the background in 1956.

GAME CHANGER – CONTAINERIZATION

Present-day container ship owned by Mediterranean Shipping Company being towed in the Houston Ship Channel.

1948

Value of tonnage passing through the Port reaches $1 billion

1950

Fireboat, *Capt Crotty*, launched at Port

Houston ranked second in U.S. for total tonnage

The 1956 arrival of the Ideal X *container ship is seen in this rendering for the cover of a 1976 Port publication.*

PORT OF HOUSTON
Magazine
MAY, 1976

Containerization was born when the world's first container ship, SS Ideal X, *sailed with 58 truck trailers from New York/New Jersey and unloaded at the Port of Houston in April 1956.*

THE CONTAINER REVOLUTION

Containerization revolutionized cargo, and it is now common to see the 20- and 40-foot metal boxes on chassis hauled by the big-rig trucks traveling area highways. The idea for standardized container cargo was developed during the 1950s. The objective was to speed the loading and unloading of cargo vessels onto and off of trucks. Rather than unloading individual pallets or cases from a cargo hold and then packing them into a truck, a crane lifts the full container from the vessel's deck and loads it directly onto a waiting truck, taking only a few minutes, or a few hours rather than several hours or a day to get freight heading to its destination. The first ship

to transport containers was an oil tanker refitted for the task by Malcom McLean in 1955. Rechristened the *SS Ideal X*, her maiden voyage was from New Jersey to Houston in April 1956. As her first port of call, Houston has the distinction of offloading history's first containers. The shipment consisted of 58 containers, 33 feet long, that were loaded onto waiting trucks at the docks and routed to delivery destinations. The *SS Ideal X* eventually left Houston with 58 trailers and 107,000 barrels of oil. While a simple first step, containerization would drive much of the Port's planning and expansion for the next 50 years and beyond.

1950
Washburn Tunnel completed

1952
Port of Houston acquired land at Barbours Cut

1953
Baytown Tunnel opened to public

The opening of the larger Panama Canal locks will allow mammoth container ships to load and unload at ports that can handle the additional ship draft and the structural requirements of larger cranes. Almost 60 years after handling 58 make-shift trailers on the inaugural container ship voyage, the Port of Houston prepares itself for the entry of container ships forecast to carry 13,800 containers or (20-foot equivalent units) TEUs, a container capacity measure, per ship. The widening and dredging of channels, re-design of older docks, added intermodal capabilities, compliant safety measurements, and the ever-present need for cooperation/coordination/innovation from Port industry partners represent a few components that come with expanded container business. The potential to double and even triple the annual amount of 2 million TEUs will become a reality and probably sooner than later.

THEN

100

NOW *A China Ocean Ship Company (COSCO) container ship enters the Port of Houston. In 2013 Maersk, the successor to McLean's Sea-Land, launched ships with a capacity of 18,000 containers. These ships are longer than the Empire State Building's occupied floors.*

THE EVOLUTION OF HEAVY LIFTING TO "DIRECT LOAD AND DISCHARGE"

Before the era of container ships, the bulk of cargo was moved by hand. Cargo handlers, known as stevedores, secured the cargo in holds and on decks using special lashings and knots. The term stevedore is Portuguese—the English translation is stuffer, as in one who stuffs ships with cargo. Eventually man-powered cranes swung pallets onto ship decks. As mechanization took hold, cranes became commonplace, leading to larger lifting devices with structurally improved wharves.

Early cargo lifting towers stand poised (on the right above) to help with heavy lifting at the Port of Houston.

BARDELLO CRANE: The highly visible "gargantuan" crane adjacent to the 610 Bridge etched the sky before being dismantled in 2013 after 17 years of dockside service at the Turning Basin.

1954
Greater Houston Metropolitan area reaches 1 million population

1956
First container ship, *Ideal X*, arrives in Houston with 58 containers

$7 million bond issue passed by 68%

DIRECT LOAD AND DISCHARGE: There has been extraordinary advancement in equipment and time-saving procedures for the purpose of immediate transport of cargo from vessel onto railroad car, road vehicle or barge.

Multi-task lifting moves pallets of cargo.

Gang rigging is secured by cargo handlers.

100 NO END TO LOAD LIFTING

Port of Houston entrance sign, 1961.

The Port launched a multi-million dollar effort for expansion in 1957 to keep pace with the shipping industry and competing ports. Step one was to acquire the Long Reach docks. At the time, Long Reach was in private hands, owned by Anderson, Clayton and Company. The company was ready to relieve itself of the expenses of operating a private wharf—a far more expensive proposition than using public wharves. If the Port could obtain this land and combine it with the more than 200 acres it recently purchased on the opposite side of the channel, then the port would have ample room to maneuver as it expanded its general cargo facilities. Bond elections showed that the public agreed with Port expansion to keep up with maritime volume and demand, by approving a Harris County Houston Ship Channel Navigation District bond issue for seven million dollars. Subsequent funding came from long-term revenue bonds in 1959 and 1961 which enabled the Port to invest more than 37 million dollars in capital improvements. These included new wharves and transit buildings, dredging (thanks to Representative Albert Thomas), promotion and development, completion of the bulk handling plant which was the biggest railroad-improvement program in the Port's history, the *M/V Sam Houston II* inspection boat, and the 12-story World Trade Building—all in the short span between 1957 and 1962.

1956

Port acquires Long Reach docks (Turning Basin)

1957

Port expands intra-railroad network

The new skyline of Houston was a majestic reflection of the maritime commerce which made it great. One third of Houston's economy stemmed from the port and ship channel, and it continued to be one of the nation's fastest growing cities in 1961 (population approximately 938,200).

1958
Port launches the *M/V Sam Houston II* (current tour boat)

1961
NASA moves headquarters to Houston/Clear Lake

1961
Hurricane Carla strikes the Texas Coast

Bulk Handling Plant Terminal completed

THE HOUSE THE PORT BUILT

100

Today, the former World Trade Center Building overlooks Minute Maid Park, home field for the Houston Astros, and operates as a 200-room luxury hotel, the Westin Houston Downtown.

The 12-story $3.5 million World Trade Center opened in 1962 in downtown Houston to serve as a center for growing international trade and cultural activities. Among those established in the new building were consulates, interpreters/translators, steamship agents, importers/exporters and the World Trade Club. It was the first building constructed specifically for that purpose. The Port of Houston's general offices abutted the World Trade Center. In 1992, the Port Authority relocated their offices to the present Port of Houston Authority building at the Turning Basin.

1962

World Trade Center opens in downtown Houston

Gathering water from the Seven Seas to officially anoint the World Trade Center, June Tellepsen, wife of chairman Howard T. Tellepsen, poured these waters into the center's reflection pool whose serpentine design was symbolic of the Houston Ship Channel.

The opening of the World Trade Building began another epic era for the Port. It was at this point that the Humble Oil Company partnered with the Port Authority to develop what became a major petrochemical and industrial complex at the Bayport Complex. For Humble Oil, the idea was to expand its petrochemical production capacity. In exchange for the port's dredging and maintaining what is now the Bayport Channel from the Houston Ship Channel to the complex, the oil company gave the Port Authority significant land to help further expand its operations.

DON'T WASTE A DROP! The Seven Seas flow into the fountain of the World Trade Center. The pitcher prominently displayed was a Blanton family heirloom brought to Texas in 1820 as members of the original Stephen F. Austin colony. W. N. Blanton was a Port Commissioner and later vice chairman from 1953–1966. His deep interest in the history of the Port was equaled only by his part in making history at the Ship Channel during those unprecedented growth years.

1963

The Humble Building completed, then the tallest building west of the Mississippi River

1964 MARKS 50 YEARS FOR THE PORT

COMMISSIONERS AND GENERAL MANAGER OF THE HARRIS COUNTY HOUSTON SHIP CHANNEL NAVIGATION DISTRICT

Seated (left to right) Vice Chairman W. N. Blanton; Chairman Howard T. Tellepsen; R. H. Pruett
Standing (left to right) E. H. Henderson; W. D. Haden II; General Manager, J. P. Turner

THE PORT CHAIRMAN SUMMARIZED THE FIRST 50 YEARS, "WE HAVE GROWN FROM THE TERMINUS OF A DREDGED-OUT MUDDY STREAM TO ONE OF THE LEADING PORTS IN THE COUNTRY AND THE WORLD."

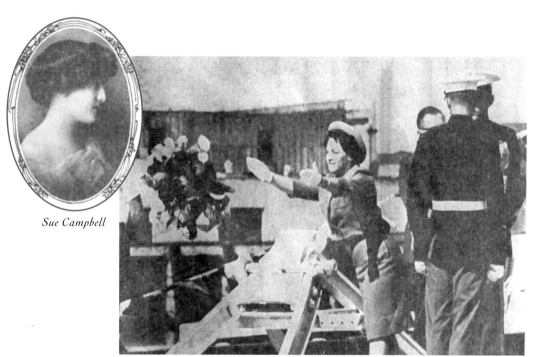

Sue Campbell

Just as her grandmother did 50 years earlier, Miss Susan Camille Lee tossed a bouquet onto the Houston Ship Channel waters and repeated "I christen thee Port of Houston." Her grandmother, Sue Campbell, was an honored guest at the ceremonies.

STEERING COMMITTEE FOR THE PORT'S 50TH BIRTHDAY CELEBRATION

The Honorable John Connally, Governor of Texas
The Honorable Bob Casey, Congressman
The Honorable Albert Thomas, Congressman
The Honorable Bill Elliott, County Judge
The Honorable Louie Welch, Mayor
Mr. John Crooker, Jr.
Mr. Leon Jaworski

Mr. Joe Allbritton
Mr. John T. Jones
Mr. William P. Hobby, Jr.
Mr. Fred Hartman
Mr. George Brown
Mr. Claud Barrett
Mr. Gus Wortham

THE IDEAL MARRIAGE OF A CITY AND THE SEA

PORT HOUSTON

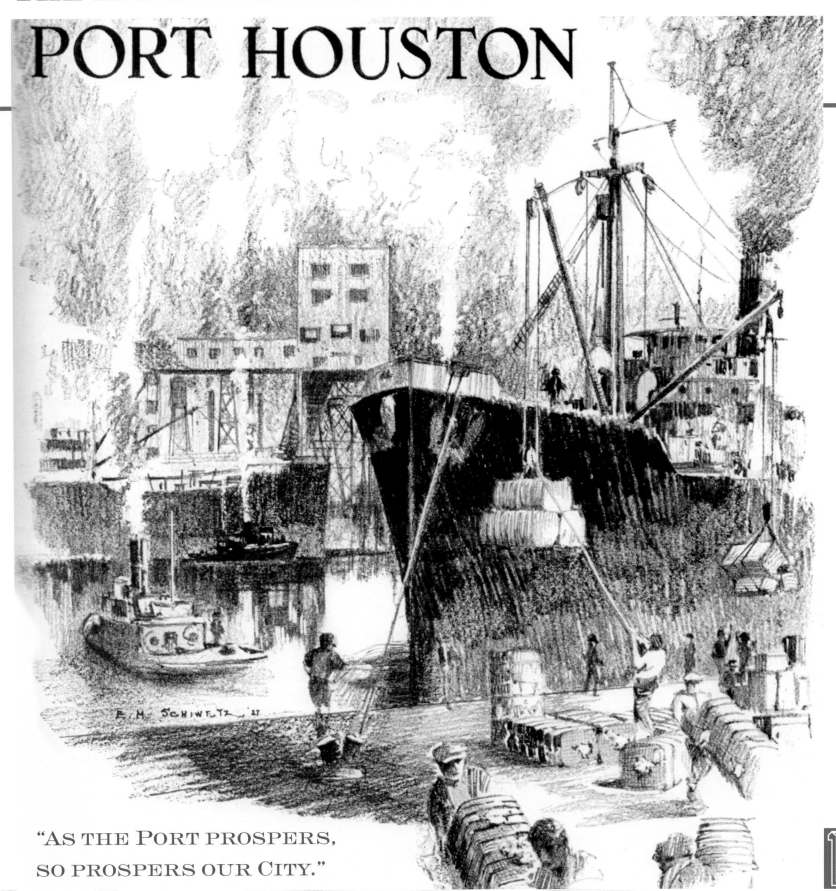

"AS THE PORT PROSPERS,
SO PROSPERS OUR CITY."

100

NASA LAUNCHES SPACE EXPLORATION

1960s NASA Space Center in Houston was made possible partly because of its proximity to a seaport—the Port of Houston. Twenty other coastal cities competed for the project.

President John F. Kennedy speaks at NASA in front of a full-scale model of the Apollo lunar landing vehicle, shown for the first time during the President's inspection trip in 1962.

The Gemini V spacecraft takes another ride following its eight-day orbital flight in 1965 as it swings off at the Port of Houston Long Reach docks.

"Houston, Tranquility Base here. The Eagle has landed." First words spoken on the moon by Astronaut Neil Armstrong (Apollo 11) in 1969.

In 1971, The Texas Legislature approved the name change from the unwieldy "Harris County Houston Ship Channel Navigation District" to "Port of Houston Authority" with expanded powers for safety, fire, and navigation control.

This scene in 1972 gives the illusion of a vessel literally sailing through a sea of bluebonnets, the official flower of Texas.

1964

50th anniversary of Port of Houston

1964

Tonnage reaches 60 million valued at $4 billion

136 million bushels of grain moves through the Port

1964

Port announces purchase of major portion of Bayport property

BERTH OF BAYPORT

It took years of negotiations and planning to move forward the new joint effort between the Port and Humble Oil, but it finally resulted in an area of land reserved for port development that included a substantial parcel of wide-open coastal prairie halfway between Morgan's Point and Kemah. The initial objective was simple—the Bayport Division, as it was called then, was to be serviced primarily by barges for general cargo, but also for tankers coming into three liquid terminals. That initial objective was met and fully in operation by 1974, 10 years after its purchase. Bayport moved millions of liquid bulk product through the Houston Ship Channel in the 1970s, 1980s, and 1990s, and would once again figure heavily in the Port's expansion plans for the next half century—in a new role.

Containerization was taking hold as evidenced by steady growth at the Barbours Cut Container Terminal, and the industry outlook was that container ship traffic was going to grow by leaps and bounds with ships getting ever bigger. To help keep pace with this kind of growing business, the Port needed to build dedicated container cargo facilities that were closer to the Gulf. After all, room had run out from the Turning Basin down Buffalo Bayou to the Lower San Jacinto Bay—Long Reach was the last possible expansion on the upper stretch of the channel. Houston was a major metropolitan area that consumed much of the area. If it wasn't Houston expanding, then it was Pasadena or La Porte or Baytown. The traditional heart of the Port of Houston operations was landlocked.

Perhaps not by grand design from the outset, but certainly as Port leadership looked toward the second half of the twentieth century and beyond, the Port had to evolve and grow to keep up. This was not going to be easy or quick. In 1998, a master plan was designed for the Bayport Container and the Cruise Terminal. Although Harris County voters approved the $387 million bond proposal to fund Phase I in 1999, ground breaking did not commence until 2004. During that time, master plan modifications were made, environmental concerns were addressed and concessions were agreed upon. Strict compliance and high standards were met as a result of this lengthy but worthwhile process. The container terminal opened in 2007, followed closely by the cruise terminal in 2008. Bayport has come a far distance since 1964 when Humble Oil and Refining sold a part of their immense West Ranch to the Port as an industrial park while developing the residential sector as Clear Lake City. This development and the offer of a large tract of land served as an inducement to NASA to locate the Manned Spacecraft Center in Houston. Today, Bayport is the most modern and environmentally sensitive container terminal in the U.S. Gulf. Former Port Authority Executive Director Dick Leach, who was active in the terminal from the very beginning, summarized Bayport's realized potential many years ago, "I have always viewed Bayport as our legacy to the future."

Excavation begins on the 1.3 mile cut at Bayport.

Bayport facility begins operations in 1974.

Clay and Liston: What Are They Really Like? Section 2, Page 1

WEATHER

HOUSTON CHRONICLE FINAL

10 Cents

Humble Plans $900 Million Bay Project

An artist's rendering of the Bayport facility vision in 1964.

100

Bayport Industrial Development, a project of Friendswood Development Company, (real estate subsidiary of Exxon Corp.) in cooperation with Port of Houston Authority, had become one of the most successful chemical industrial developments in the country by 1984. Coupled with its sibling terminal, Barbours Cut, Bayport has become the second leg of container development on the Port assuring advancement in the 21st century.

1965

The Astrodome opens as the 8th wonder of the world

Port purchases Long Reach Docks

Bayport Terminal with tanker in the foreground, container facility adjacent, and petroleum storage at the top. In addition to Bayport's diversity in handling liquid petroleum, containers (capacity of 2.3 million TEUs), and cruise ships (Princess Cruises and Norwegian Cruise Lines), its environmental benefits include the preservation of 956 acres of coastal habitat, 173 acres of wetlands, and preservation of a 128-acre buffer zone.

1966

First container crane in the Gulf Coast delivered to Houston

1969

Apollo 11 lands on the moon

"Houston" is first word spoken from the lunar surface

Container movement happens around the clock at Bayport Terminal.

1969

Houston Intercontinental Airport, now named George H. W. Bush
Intercontinental Airport, is opened to the public

1971

Shell Oil Company relocates corporate headquarters to Houston. More than 200 major firms move
headquarters, subsidiaries and divisions here in the years following

THE HOUSTON SHIP CHANNEL BRIDGE

Autos fly over the 610 Bridge above the Turning Basin Terminal with containers stacked neatly in the foreground and petrochemical presence providing a fluorescent background.

Sidney Sherman Bridge, named for the courageous commander in the Battle of San Jacinto who also commissioned the first survey of the Houston Ship Channel, was approved in 1964 for the cost of 12 million dollars and completed in 1973. Also known as the 610 Bridge, or The Ship Channel Bridge, it is seen above with the Houston skyline in the background.

The 610 Bridge had a detection system installed to warn too-tall ships from passing under it in later years.

BARBOURS CUT BEGINS

Barbours Cut dates back to the 1920s when a gentleman named Captain Barbour decided that he could best the Port of Houston, or at least nip at its heels. He carved out a canal and built docks located right at Morgan's Cut. His idea was to get freighters to offload at his facility rather than steam further up the channel to Houston. The idea had merit, but its weakness was timing. Just when it was up and running, the Crash of 1929 sealed the operation's fate; it was never able to make a profit. The other glitch in Barbour's thinking was getting the cargo from his docks to the rail hub. Houston's wharves already had facilities and direct rail. The reality was that a terminal at Barbours Cut was a good idea, just premature.

It was in the early 1970s that planning shifted into high gear for the Port's use of Barbours Cut as a container terminal. Port Commission Chairman Fentress Bracewell (1970–1985) championed the merits of this risky venture from the beginning, realizing that container growth was of the "now." The Port of Houston took the lead in fusing containerization with shipping, despite a slow acceptance with ports in the Gulf. A boon to the completion of the Barbours Cut terminal was convincing the container shipping company Sea-Land to move from its wharf at the Turning Basin to Barbours Cut. Not only was Barbours Cut tailored for SeaLand's needs, it was also closer to the Gulf, which allowed ships to spend half the time navigating the Houston Ship Channel in and out of port.

First Lighter Aboard Ship (LASH) vessel at Barbours Cut in 1972. These long vessels carried barges of different sizes to ports less developed for the loaded barges to be pushed up rivers. The LASH berth at Barbour's Cut now functions as a lay berth after 20 years as a LASH dock.

The gamble that was Barbours Cut yielded dividends that continue today. This terminal catapulted the Port to the forefront of container activity in the Gulf Coast. This bold endeavor was symbolic of visionary and energetic leadership that has endured for over 100 years.

Barbours Cut Terminal was designed to permit container, LASH, and roll-on/roll-off (RoRo) cargo to be handled quickly. RoRo ships are vessels designed to carry wheeled cargo, such as automobiles, trucks, semi-trailer trucks, trailers, and railroad cars, that are driven on and off the ship on their own wheels. This is in contrast to lift-on/lift-off (LoLo) vessels, which use a crane to load and unload cargo.

Barbours Cut Container Terminal is in constant motion along its 6,000 feet of continuous quay with Panamax Cranes loading trucks driven by mobile-app savvy drivers.

When it opened in 1977, the original capacity of Barbours Cut was 1 million 20-foot equivalent units (TEUs). A TEU is equal to a single 20-foot container, whereas 40-foot containers are considered two 20-foot unit equivalents. Before later expansions, the facility's traffic grew to handle 1.6 million TEUs per year. Much of the credit goes to the men and women who worked the Barbours Cut Terminal. They kept containers moving without fail.

As containerization grew, Barbours Cut quickly became crucial to the Port. The vision of a Bayport container terminal with the most up-to-date facilities was developed by new leadership on the Port Commission. During his tenure of 15 years, Chairman Bracewell partnered with Port Executive Directors George W. Altvater, Richard P. Leach, and James D. Pugh to grow the Port's reputation as a world port leader while increasing the economic value of the Port to Houston and the entire state of Texas.

Ned S. Holmes took the reins as Chairman in 1988 and guided the Port with vision and determination. Environmental opposition, labor disputes, revenue losses, public apathy, railway glitches, and a host of other issues were encountered by this administration. Similiar to the past leadership, perseverance and vision prevailed. Holmes led successful bond elections resulting in a wider and deeper Houston Ship Channel while setting an environmental precedent in the preservation of Galveston Bay. The Port Authority also acquired Jacintoport, Care, Woodhouse, Public Elevator No. 2, and built a cruise terminal at Barbours Cut.

Barbours Cut Container Terminal began operations in 1977 as the first public terminal in Texas to handle standardized cargo containers. The terminal has also handled RoRo and project cargo (equipment) across its 250 acres of paved marshaling area and 255,000 square feet of warehouse space.

1971

Port of Houston Authority becomes official title

1972

Barbours Cut Lash Dock operations open

LANDMARK NAMING

Barbours Cut was officially named Fentress Bracewell Barbours Cut Container Terminal in 1988. This facility was named after the longest serving Chairman of the Port Commission who helped develop the terminal.

1973

The Arab Oil Embargo causes demand for Texas oil to boom

1973

Houston International Seafarers Center opens at Turning Basin

1973

Sidney Sherman Bridge (610 Bridge over Turning Basin) opens

Day and night container activity at Barbours Cut is a common sight.

1974
Bayport Channel dedication

1977
Barbours Cut begins container terminal operations

1981
Kathryn J. Whitmire is elected as the first woman mayor of Houston

VICE PRESIDENT BUSH VISITS HIS HOME PORT TO PRESENT AWARD

"I'm pleased to be here today to represent President Reagan in honoring the Port of Houston Authority for its contributions to the export promotion effort of the United States. As a Houstonian, I'm proud to say that the Port of Houston is one of the nation's leading ports. With its ongoing program of capital improvements, it has provided facilities to serve all facets of our country's export trade. Over the past four years alone, exports through the Port have increased 73 percent by value and 54 percent by tonnage.

This hasn't been the result of mere luck or accident. The Port of Houston Authority has conducted an aggressive international marketing campaign to further its aims. It has provided assistance, advice, consultation and information on all aspects of exporting to encourage and promote international trade. It has served as host and co-host for briefing programs, seminars and trade missions designed to expand international trade.

And of singular importance, this World Trade Week in Houston, it has operated a World Trade Center as a focal point for international business. In addition, the Port Authority has hosted overseas visitors and conducted overseas trade development trips and kept the shipping community informed of developments and opportunities in international trade through The Port of Houston Magazine and a comprehensive advertising program.

This export record was noted by the President's "E" Award Committee when it recommended the Port of Houston Authority for the President's "E" Award. Since 1961, this award has served as recognition of and an incentive for American business and industry to increase exports and help offset our severe imbalance of payments.

It is hoped that through this Award, the Port of Houston Authority's performance will set an example for American firms and organizations everywhere to follow in helping to meet the economic challenge now facing our country.

In the name and by the authority of the President of the United States, I now have the honor to present the "E" Award for Export Service to Mr. Fentress Bracewell, Chairman of the Port of Houston Authority.

With this certificate comes the famous big blue "E" pennant. May you display it with the knowledge that you've made a significant contribution to our nation's economic growth and that your contribution has been recognized and appreciated.

Congratulations!"

Vice President Bush presents the President's "E Star Award" for Export Leadership in 1981 to Port Authority Chairman Fentress Bracewell. The Port of Houston received this award again in 2008.

In one rendering, three important eras of the Houston Ship Channel are depicted. The San Jacinto Monument, located at the site where Texas independence was won, marks the first moment when Buffalo Bayou provided vital service to her residents. The battleship Texas *was commissioned the same year as the Ship Channel opened, and her years of active naval service paralleled a period of great expansion for the Port of Houston. Finally, the cargo ship, M.V. Tactician, featuring its patented heavy lift derrick amidship, arrives in the 1960s laden with goods from Liverpool, itself a symbol of commerce; the vision that has always been the Houston Ship Channel and the Port of Houston, one and the same.*

1981

Double stack train container transport began in Houston

1982

Beltway 8 Bridge (Jesse H. Jones Memorial Bridge) opens

1983

Hurricane Alicia hits Houston and Galveston

HOUSTON INTERNATIONAL SEAFARERS CENTER

The Houston International Seafarers Center opened in 1973 and serves seafarers from all corners of the world as they visit the Port of Houston. Their spiritual, recreational, and human needs are met by chaplains who furnish them with a "home away from home."

Friends gather and dine at the Seafarers Center.

Father Rivers Patout, the "Dean of Port Chaplains," for 46 years, displays his maritime vestments.

The Lou Lawler Seafarers Center in La Porte, Texas, is located across the street from Barbours Cut Terminal. The Center opened in 1993 to accommodate the expanding operations at Barbours Cut.

Howard T. Tellepsen Seafarers Center, at the Turning Basin Terminal Houston, Texas, has served as a virtual seafarer's YMCA.

Located in the heart of the Turning Basin, the Howard T. Tellepsen Seafarers Center is a safe and hospitable retreat for all seamen passing through Port of Houston waters. The organization was formed by the joint efforts and support of the Port Commission, the Port community, and the Greater Houston area, serving as the first ecumenical Seafarers Center in the world.

JESSE H. JONES MEMORIAL BRIDGE

Traffic along the Houston Ship Channel was not disrupted during construction. The bridge is two miles long and at the time of completion was America's longest cast-in-place, segmentally-constructed, box-girder span bridge.

In 1982 the Beltway 8 Toll Bridge opened and was officially named the Jesse H. Jones Memorial Bridge in honor of the most influential businessman and philanthropist in Houston's history. When identifying their location, Houston Pilots call the toll bridge the "two dollah bridge" in reference to the toll fee.

PORT TERMINAL RAILROAD ASSOCIATION

The Port Terminal Railroad Association (PTRA) was established in 1924 to control public belt railway service on equal terms to all channel industries as a neutral organization. The publicly owned railroad stretched for 72 miles in 1930 and presently consists of 154 miles of track in addition to maintaining 20 bridges while serving seven yards.

PTRA handles chemicals, grain, plastic, coke, fuel, steel, food products, industrial products, intermodal, dimensional loads and autos. By way of its rail interchange network, PTRA originates and terminates shipments from each of the continental 48 states as well as Mexico and Canada.

Southern Pacific's electronically-controlled gravity switching yard at Houston moved freight faster and kept pace with 1966 Space Age.

1983	1984	1989
Free Trade Zones (FTZ) established throughout the Port	Wharf Number 32 completed at Turning Basin	Jacintoport Terminal opened featuring its Spiralveyor

CONTAINERS DOUBLE STACK ON THE TRACK

In 1981, the innovative and highly cost effective development of stacking containers two-high on rail cars began in Houston. The first transportation route was from Houston to Los Angeles.

DESERT SHIELD / STORM

Acres of ground combat equipment poised for military transport to another continent.

1989

Port of Houston 8th busiest port in the world

Port of Houston is first in foreign tonnage in U.S.

1990

The Beneficial Uses Group (BUG) was formed to develop environmentally innovative and beneficial ways to use dredge material from the Houston Ship Channel

Houston was a leading port of exit and entry for equipment used in the Middle East during Operation Desert Storm. Between August 1990 and December 1991 the Fentress Bracewell Barbours Cut Container Terminal handled nearly 460,000 tons of military cargo, including 38,000 vehicles. The military shipments accounted for more than 100 vessel calls during the 16-month period. The Port of Houston was the third largest load center for the U.S. military and ranked second in the nation in the number of ships handled.

THE WORLD IS OUR TRADING PARTNER

Change came to the Port of Houston in the 1980s, and the Port Commission worked to affect that change by being accessible to all stakeholders—labor, maritime industry, environmental groups, and the Corps of Engineers. Through collaboration with these groups, positive results became apparent. Hard decisions were made to ensure profitability and secure long-term growth. One of these difficult decisions was to close the World Trade Building after more than 26 years of service to consolidate the expanding Port offices to a newly constructed building on Port grounds at the Turning Basin. International field offices were opened with strategic foreign trade partners to foster world trade.

Strong foreign trade continued with Canada and Mexico but sights were set on increased international trade with our neighbors in Central and South America along with fast developing countries in Asia and Africa. European commerce grew from more demand of goods, larger ports, bigger ships, and advanced technology. This trend has gained momentum over the years to establish Houston as the top U.S. market for exports. In 2012, Houston's leading trading partners were Mexico, Canada, Venezuela, Saudi Arabia, Brazil, China, Columbia, The Netherlands, Russia, Germany and Nigeria.

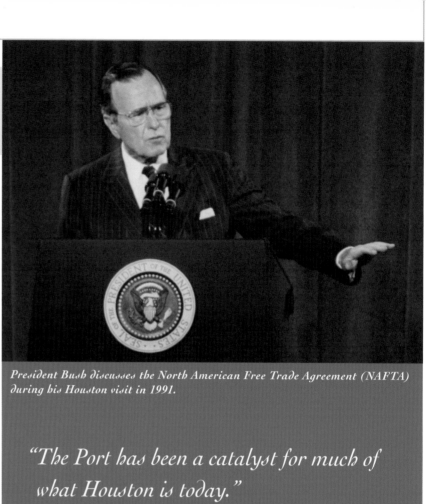

President Bush discusses the North American Free Trade Agreement (NAFTA) during his Houston visit in 1991.

"The Port has been a catalyst for much of what Houston is today."

– PRESIDENT GEORGE H. W. BUSH

Even in this 1924 cover of a Port publication, the importance of international trade was emphasized.

The Port's dedication to world trade is illustrated in this 1992 advertisement. Research shows that the Port and the industries along the Houston Ship Channel combined are responsible for approximately one-third of every dollar generated in Houston.

A New Home for The Port of Houston Authority

Flags were unfurled by the wind at the opening of Port of Houston Authority Building.

The anchor symbolizes the Port of Houston Authority Building's maritime cornerstone.

In 1991, the Port of Houston Authority completed its new Executive Office Building centralizing three office locations into one modern building located at the Turning Basin.

100

FRED HARTMAN BRIDGE

The Fred Hartman Bridge or Baytown Bridge is a 2.6 mile-long cable-stayed bridge spanning the Houston Ship Channel with a minimum 530 foot bottom width to accommodate larger ships. The bridge was named for Fred Harman (1908–1991), longtime editor and publisher of the *Baytown Sun* from 1950 to 1974. Fred Hartman Bridge opened in 1995 at a cost of $117.5 million. It replaced the Baytown Tunnel which had to be removed when the Houston Ship Channel was deepened to 45 feet.

1991

New Port of Houston Authority Building opened at Turning Basin

1992

Public Elevator No. 2 opened with 6.2 million bushel capacity

PORT OF HOUSTON AUTHORITY TERMINALS

When Port Commission Chairman Jim Edmonds began his tenure in 2000, the Port had reversed revenues from losses to earnings of $100 million. The Bayport Terminal opened in 2007 and catapulted the Port's container tonnage figures and revenues. The facility's annual capacity will eventually be 7,000 TEUs, strongly contributing to the Port Authority's 2013 revenues, which hovered around $200 million per year in addition to its $1.6 billion impact on the region's economy.

Approaching the centennial as a deep-water port and home to over 150 terminals, the Port of Houston managed to overcome repeated challenges from geography, nature, economies, war, and politics. Yet the Port is at another pivotal juncture in its history—emergent patterns mirror conditions facing Houston in 1914.

TURNING BASIN TERMINAL

This terminal is the navigational head of the Houston Ship Channel and includes the City Docks, former Long Reach Docks, Wharf 32, a heavy load freight handling facility containing 20 acres of heavy duty marshaling area, and Manchester Terminal, a liquid bulk facility.

PUBLIC ELEVATOR NO. 2

The fully-automated Public Elevator No. 2 has a capacity of 6.2 bushels with a remarkable loading speed of 120,000 bushels per hour and located adjacent to Woodhouse Terminal.

WOODHOUSE TERMINAL

Purchased in 1993 (formerly Goodpasture) by the Port and located in Galena Park near Sims Bayou, this break-bulk facility has three cargo wharves and covered warehouse space.

BULK MATERIALS HANDLING PLANT

Completed in 1962, this Port-owned dry bulk export/import facility is located at Greens Bayou and equipped with a sophisticated dust collection system and high-speed loading systems to enhance intermodal transportation between ship and rail/truck.

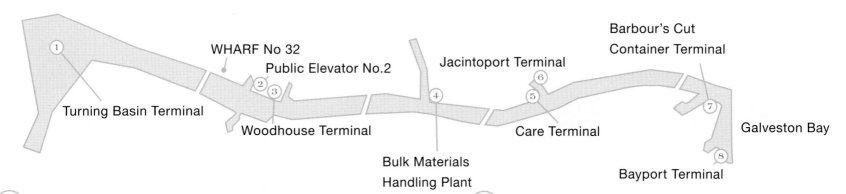

Barbour's Cut
Container Terminal

WHARF No 32

Public Elevator No.2

Jacintoport Terminal

Turning Basin Terminal

Woodhouse Terminal

Care Terminal

Galveston Bay

Bulk Materials
Handling Plant

Bayport Terminal

CARE TERMINAL

Located near Channelview, this terminal was bought by the Port Authority in 1995 and is designed for handling project cargo and heavy lift cargo. The grain elevator in the background is privately owned and operated.

JACINTOPORT TERMINAL

The Port Authority acquired this terminal in 1989 located near Channelview across from Care Terminal. It was the first automated facility (formerly named Omniport) of its kind. It features the "Spiralveyor" bagged handling system that loads/unloads ships rapidly and is complemented by on-site bagging equipment that packages corn, oats, rice, soybeans, wheat, and other food products.

BARBOUR'S CUT CONTAINER TERMINAL

The Port Authority purchased the land in 1952 and developed it in 1972 with the opening of its LASH dock, followed by container berths, roll-off/roll-on ramps, and acres of marshaling/storage area.

BAYPORT TERMINAL

Bayport became the property of the Port Authority in 1964 and the adjoining Bayport Industrial District quickly ascended to one of the most successful chemical industrial developments in the country. Deep-water arrived in 1977 with a 1,600 foot square turning basin at its head. The container terminal opened in 2008, followed by the cruise terminal in 2009.

M.V. SAM HOUSTON II, "SHOW WINDOW OF THE PORT"

First Port Commission inspection boat, 1929

(Photo by Calvin Wheat)

Port of Houston inspection yacht, Sam Houston I, *1949*

School children learn port ecology on the Sam Houston *as part of the "Floating School" program. Integration of education, good citizenship, and the outdoors is promoted at the Port.*

Launched in 1958, the M/V Sam Houston II *hosted a million passengers by 1979.*

1993

Lou Lawler Seafarers Center opened in La Porte

Woodhouse Terminal acquired by the Port

1993

Port announces purchase of additional Bayport property

City Zoning defeated for the third time

1995

Fred Hartman Bridge opened to public

Care Terminal acquired by the Port

The M/V Sam Houston II *glows in the channel lights at dusk on the Houston Ship Channel. The 98-foot long inspection boat with 24-foot base was commissioned in 1958 at a cost of $300,000.*

1997

Baytown Tunnel removed

Barbours Cut Cruise Terminal opens

1999

Port reaches milestone 1 million TEUs (containers) per year

1999

Bond approved for first phase at Bayport Terminals

MARITIME EDUCATION

The Texas Clipper II, *Texas A&M University at Galveston's (TAMUG) training vessel, sails with students aboard.*

TAMUG houses the Texas Maritime Academy which prepares graduates for licensing as officers in the American Merchant Marine.

San Jacinto College Maritime Technical & Training Center, located near Bayport, breaks ground in 2014 and will provide education for careers in the maritime industry.

Port employees Dana Blume and Liz Johnson were Junior Achievement volunteers at HISD's Port Houston Elementary School. Students show their Certificates of Achievement, a result of partnership with the Port of Houston Authority.

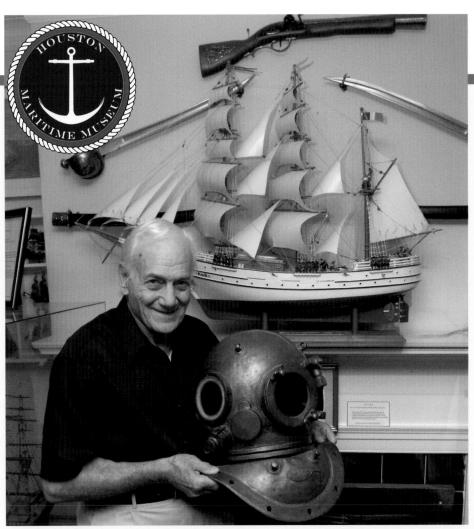

Founder Jim Manzolillo displayed maritime artifacts at the Houston Maritime Museum. These represent our rich history reflected in its mission statement, "To capture and preserve the wonder and influence of maritime history and the maritime industry with focus on the development of Houston, the Texas Gulf Coast, and the State of Texas."

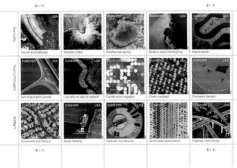

A FOREVER stamp depicting a pair of towboats owned by Houston-based Kirby Corp & Enterprise Marine "wrangling" commercial barges on the Houston Ship Channel made quite a splash, since it was the first time a Houston landmark has appeared on a postage stamp. Its title "Barge Fleeting" was part of Earthscapes, a series of 15 stamps selected from 40,000 proposals considered by the U.S. Postal Service in 2012.

Vice President Biden and Chairman Longoria at Bayport surrounded by dignitaries including Paul Jaenichen of the U.S. Department of Transportation Maritime Administration (MARAD), Congressman Green, Secretary Foxx, Port Executive Director Waterworth, Commissioner Fitzgerald and Congresswoman Lee in 2013.

VIP's
"VISITORS IN PORT"

100

Queen Elizabeth and Prince Phillip accompanied by Mayor Kathy Whitmire visit in 1992.

Chairman Ned Holmes welcomes Eduard Shevardnadze, the President of Republic of Georgia, in 1999.

Chairman Archie Bennett greets Prince Charles from the royal family of Great Britain during his visit in 1986.

Harald V, King of Norway, visits with Chairman Edmonds on the Sam Houston *in 2005.*

Executive Director Tom Kornegay introduces the President of Panama, Martin Torrijos, in 2006.

ABOVE AND BELOW

Historical Norwegian Windjammer *visits in 1980.*

Tall Ship Golden Hinde *is a replica of Sir Francis Drake's warship and was open to the public at the battleground in 1989.*

Tall Ship Elissa, *built in 1877, visits the Bayport Terminal.*

TALL SHIPS AND A NAMESAKE SUBMARINE VISIT THE PORT

Mayor Kathy Whitmire presents a plaque to Captain Mensch of the USS Houston.

Nuclear submarine USS Houston *rises with lifting towers on the horizon.*

USS Houston, *with escorts, visits the Port of Houston in 1983.*

ALL ABOARD! CRUISE SHIPS SAIL FROM HOUSTON

The first cruise ship, Lafayette, *sailed annually from Houston to the West Indies in 1924 and 1925.*

M/V Norwegian Star *leaves Barbours Cut Terminal initiating a luxury cruise line service from Houston to the Caribbean (Texaribbean Service) in 1997.*

Passengers embark onto Disney's The Big Red Boat *in 2000.*

The Norwegian Cruise line Norwegian Sea *at Barbours Cut.*

Hurricane Ike caused devastation with 100 mph winds and flood waters which rendered Galveston's Cruise Terminal inoperable in September 2008. In the wake of that storm, Carnival Cruise Lines requested the Port of Houston to receive its two cruise ships at the new and unfinished Bayport Cruise Terminal. Bayport was thrust into action and opened four days later to accommodate more than 5,000 passengers and assisted in keeping the cruise line business in the Texas region.

BATTLESHIPS AND SPACESHIPS

100

USS San Jacinto, *a U.S. Navy guided missile cruiser of the Aegis Class and the third ship named after the San Jacinto Battleground. Vice President George H. W. Bush commissioned this ship at Wharf No. 32 in 1988. He served on the second namesake ship, a light aircraft carrier, during World War II.*

USS Stout, *a guided missile destroyer, built in 1992 at a cost of $880 million, is dressed for its visit. This practice of decorating a naval vessel is performed for special occasions by stringing dressing lines between the masts (and down to the ensign and jack staffs), and displaying national flags at the mastheads.*

USS Cape St. George, *Navy missile frigate docks at the Woodhouse Terminal.*

SPACE SHUTTLE REPLICA EXPLORER RETURNS TO HOUSTON

On June 1, 2013, the Houston Ship Channel once again played an important role in space exploration history when it welcomed the space shuttle replica, *Explorer*, as it sailed on a barge to Clear Lake. It was later moved into position at its new home at Space Center Houston, a visitor's center for NASA's Johnson Space Center.

NASA originally selected Clear Lake City in Houston for the site of the Johnson Space Center because of its proximity to the Port of Houston and the Houston Ship Channel. U.S. Vice President Lyndon Baines Johnson, as the chairman of the National Space Committee, likely aided in selecting a location in Texas. Historian Stephen B. Oates analyzed the reasons for Houston's selection. "But the truly deciding factor was not political pressure. It was the winning combination of advantages which Houston itself had to offer. Chief among these was the fact that Houston's ship channel and port facilities provided an excellent means for transporting bulky space vehicles to other NASA locations, chiefly Cape Canaveral," Oates said.

FREE RIDE HOME: As a contribution to the community in support of its space heritage, Kirby Corp donated transport services of this Explorer *replica from Cape Canaveral to Space Center Houston in Clear Lake, a 1,200-nautical-mile trip.*

NOW AS THEN

Future generations might well look back on the Port of Houston and the Houston Ship Channel as one of the great wonders of the modern world—perhaps even on a scale with the Seven Wonders of the Ancient World. It is, after all, epic when you consider that it was really the citizenry that drove the multi-generational effort to achieve a deep-water channel for a city 52 miles inland on the banks of what was little more than a dark water creek that meandered to a shallow bay an average height man could wade across at low tide. A century ago, the mere idea was inconceivable.

Well into 1914, the issues facing Houston's port were moving commerce straight into Houston via a channel deep enough for ocean-going vessels; capitalizing on a budding petroleum industry that was ignited by the gushers at Spindletop; and fully utilizing the rail and transportation capabilities of shipping and manufacturing facilities that multiplied at breakneck speed. And we've come full circle.

100

"The bayou which leads from Houston to Galveston is overhung by lofty and graceful magnolias; and in the season of their blossoming, one may sail for miles along the channel with the heavy, passionate fragrance of the queen flower drifting about him. This bayou Houston hopes one day to widen and dredge all the way to Galveston; but its prettiness and romance will then be gone."

— EDWARD KING, 1873

2001
Following 9/11, Port initiates industry-leading security measures

Today, as the light of 2014 shines on Houston, shale oil and gas are re-energizing American commerce. For the first time in many decades, the United States expects to enjoy the benefits of being an energy exporter, thereby reducing American interests in politically unstable areas. Houston and the Port are home to the largest petrochemical complex in the United States—responsible for more than 40 percent of the country's fuel that supplies cars, trucks and aircraft, including all of the military grade jet fuel. Profound amounts of tonnage in plastics and industrial chemicals and gases originate along the channel—in some cases up to 50 percent of national capacity. Companies that provide vital products, equipment, and know-how to find, drill, and service oil and gas wells are predominantly located in Houston and on the channel from near the Turning Basin all the way down to Bolivar.

In addition to petrochemical and related products, a myriad of other cargo contributes to the port ranking as number two in the U.S. for total cargo tonnage, and number one in foreign cargo. The Port generates a million jobs and is part of nearly $200 billion in state economic activity, and as much as $500 billion in United States economic activity. Combined, all this swells up to a massive economic impact to America from the Port of Houston—underscoring a tagline of "Most Irreplaceable Port."

Oil tanker deck carries miles of piping.

After World War II, development of the petrochemical industry along the Houston Ship Channel accelerated and transformed the Port of Houston into the nation's largest petrochemical production complex and the second largest in the world. Vopak Terminal (pictured above), located in Deer Park, exemplifies the size of mammoth tank storage providers specializing in the storage and handling of liquid chemicals, gases, and oil products on the ship channel.

THE PETROCHEMICAL CAPITAL OF THE UNITED STATES

In 1984, 25 percent of the country's petroleum refining capacity and 50 percent of the United States' petrochemical production capacity was located on the banks of the Houston Ship Channel. In 2014, Houston is the petrochemical capital of the U.S. and second largest in the world to Rotterdam, with 38 percent of the nation's refining capacity.

SIZE MATTERS

Today, as in 1914, port leaders keep a careful watch on vessel size, and part of the ship size issue may be affected by the Panama Canal. When the canal opened, it resulted in some traffic to the Houston Ship Channel. Today, the Panama Canal is being expanded once again to accommodate larger ships, and some of these larger vessels have already begun visiting the Port of Houston.

Post-Panamax ships are at the forefront of the size issue. Even with the refit of larger locks, these container ships are too massive to pass through the Panama Canal. Indeed, they are practically man-made islands, with some exceeding 1,300 feet and requiring a depth of more than 50 feet. The only cargo vessels requiring deeper draft are the Chinamax ships at 79 feet, but they are largely limited to Far East and West Coast ports. For the Houston Ship Channel, specifically the main stem from Bolivar to the two container terminals at Barbour's Cut and Bayport Terminal will later in 2014 be at the depth of 45 feet—five feet short of the 50 feet needed for the largest ships to enter the channel. Because these ships can carry between 11,000 and 14,500 TEUs, the Port must resolve this seeming conundrum to avert stagnation.

A 1999 RIBBON CUTTING CELEBRATION: It took 30 years to receive Congressional approval and funding for widening the channel from 400 feet to 530 and deepening from 40 feet to 45. The project was completed in 2005. The cost-benefit ratio of this critical project is a $5 benefit for every $1 spent. Oil tankers can increase their cargo of 70,000 tons of crude oil to 95,000 tons. The dredge material was used to create 4,250 acres of marshland while rebuilding historical islands that were eroding from storms.

Chains loom large to the last link.

Issues such as dredging deeper, wider and further into the Gulf require consideration, as they impact future industrial development, maritime operations and the environment. Some of the new ships on the drawing boards may be just too big to be accommodated by an ever-deepening channel, a process that would necessitate carving even farther past Bolivar.

2001
Tropical Storm Allison causes widespread flooding in the Houston area. The storm is called a 500-year event

2003
Norwegian Cruise Line sails from Barbours Cut

The seemingly endless deck length of this tanker in port exceeds the total height of the 64-story Williams Tower (formerly Transco Tower).
This RoRo vehicle carrier ship (below) dwarfs the docks below with its massive size.

A MUTUAL PARTNERSHIP

In the days before the ship channel, the ports of Houston and Galveston were slugging it out, trying to get shipmasters or owners to use their facilities. Although Galveston was winning at the time, ship owners were complaining that the Galveston Wharf Company was charging exorbitant fees. As described earlier, Houston had a response. It sent barges out into the bay to meet the cargo ships. The deal was that they could offload their cargo more cheaply onto the barges than doing so at the Galveston wharves. The barges brought the goods back to the original Houston docks downtown and sent them on their merry way—either by train or wagon cart or mule. It's not implausible to think of transfer stations resembling offshore production platforms that move the containers from the New Panamax vessels onto conventional ships that can easily navigate the lower stem of the Houston Ship Channel to the Barbour's Cut or Bayport Terminals.

During the Fifties and Sixties, containerization helped speed loading and unloading ships. In later decades, the addition of Barbour's Cut and the Bayport development increased handling capacity tremendously. Bayport still has some expansion left in the plan and Barbour's Cut is being upgraded as well. What's left?

2004

First modern light rail line (7.5 miles)
begins operations in Houston

2004

PHA sought out and received federal security grants and opened the Port
Coordination Center to enhance communication

2005

Hurricane Katrina devastates
New Orleans

A new generation of cranes headed to Bayport in 2006.

THE SPEED OF COMMERCE

A visionary will come along to solve the ship size issue. That's always been a blessing on the Port of Houston—someone with "the big idea" manages to show up right when needed. But still remaining is the need to increase traffic within the channel in order to move more goods, thereby increasing revenues and keeping the Port strategically important while positioning it for continued growth and traffic.

A crucial part of the equation is handling the cargo once it hits dry land. Again, one of the things that Houston had going for it in 1914 was its rail hub. Lines radiated from the city in almost every direction, making the city an ideal distribution center. That hasn't changed. Now, however, it is part of that great network coordinating the efforts of the Texas Department of Transportation (TxDOT), city and county planners, and petroleum and industrial complexes lining the channel and the Galveston Bay. It's not just ships and docks. Trucking, rail, air, and sea—Houston has a commerce network that moves products from here to there and back. Moving the goods is no problem in and of itself, but the name of the game is speed. That is at the center of growth and vitality for the Port of Houston—and one answer lies in turn time. Getting ships into and out of port faster is imperative. Time in-port is time lost for shippers and lost sales opportunities for those waiting on their goods to sell. Ned Holmes, having served as Port Commission Chairman for many years, as well as having served on the TxDOT commission, understood the bigger picture—the maneuvers that all components of commerce must engage in to fuel this large consumptive engine called the economy. Improved highways in and out of the port terminals, fast lane access out of the heart of the city to the toll road networks, and circumventing Houston-proper congestion by traversing the future segments of the Grand Parkway will help get cargo into and out of the Port.

2005
Houston Ship Channel completes 30-year project: 530' wide, 45' deep

2007
Houston Ship Channel Security District formed per Texas State Legislature

2007
$250 million bond issue passed by 65%

2007

Bayport Container
Terminal begins operations

2008

World's first port certified ISO 28000:2007
for security management

LOAD CENTER OF THE U.S. GULF

Spiralveyor at Jacinto Port handles 350 to 400 tons of baggage per hour.

Ship to shore cranes

Barge boom crane

Endless pallets of bagged rice cargo

2008
Hurricane Ike hits Houston
and Galveston

2008
Bayport Cruise Terminal Building opens
to assist after Hurricane Ike

2010
Port adds *Yellow Rose* to fleet of Pilot vessels

TEU SPELLS CONTAINER
(TWENTY-FOOT EQUIVALENT UNIT)

Exported TEUs leave the Port of Houston.

WHAT IS HOUSTON SENDING IN THOSE CONTAINERS?

1. 30% - Resins and Plastics
2. 30% - Machinery, Appliances and Electronics
3. 14% - Chemicals and Minerals
4. 7% - Food and Drink
5. 6% - Automobiles
6. 3% - Steel and Metals
7. 3% - Retail Consumer Goods
8. 3% - Apparel and Accessories
9. 2% - Hardware and Construction Materials
10. 2% - Fabrics and Raw Cotton

WHAT IS IN THOSE IMPORTED CONTAINERS?

1. 20% - Food and Drink
2. 13% - Machinery, Appliances and Electronics
3. 12% - Steel and Metals
4. 12% - Hardware and Construction Materials
5. 10% - Retail Consumer Goods
6. 9% - Chemicals and Minerals
7. 7% - Resins and Plastics
8. 6% - Furniture
9. 6% - Automobiles
10. 5% - Apparel and Accessories

Imported TEUs are neatly arranged for the road trip to their destination.

PIPE DREAMS

The oil and petrochemical industries assure a steady flow of piping for both vertical and horizontal exploration.

Acres of steel and piping are stored in marshaling areas for rapid transport.

Cargo not moved in a container is referred to as "break bulk." As the nation's leading break bulk port, the Port of Houston's general cargo terminals handle about 65 percent of the break bulk cargo in the U.S. Their high-speed efficiency loading equipment handles a large range of cargo from steel to finer gradients of proppants, which is bagged granules of ceramics and silica sand used in the process of hydraulic fracturing for shale oil and gas well exploration.

Nacelle units travel by truck and rail. A nacelle is the encasement housing for nearly 8,000 generating components in the wind turbine assembly.

The massive rotors of wind turbine generators are gently transferred at the Port.

WIND POWER STRUCTURES SAIL THROUGH THE PORT

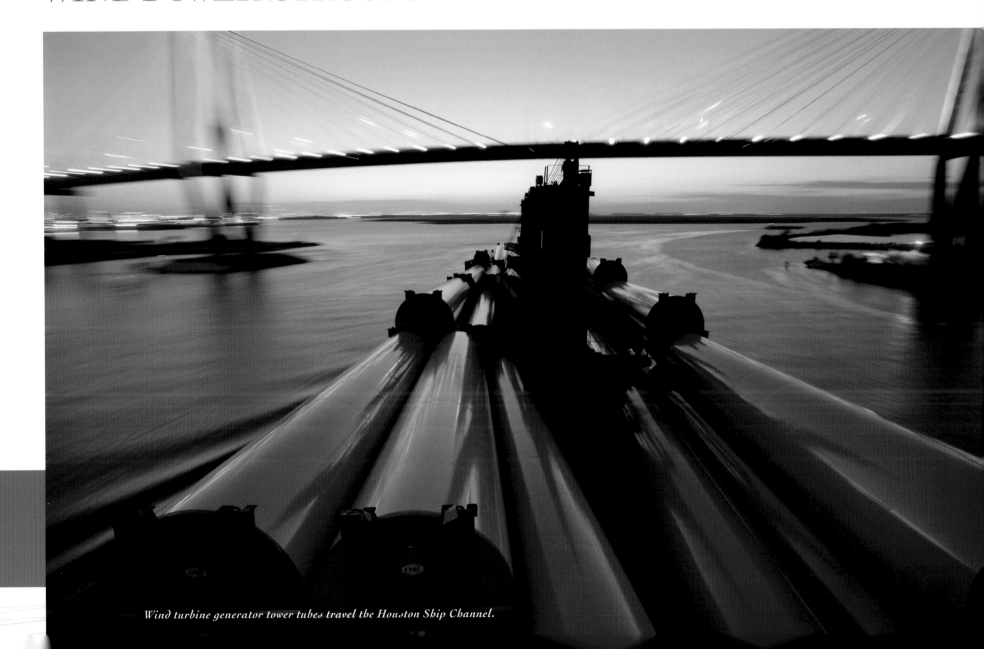

Wind turbine generator tower tubes travel the Houston Ship Channel.

THE PERIL OF FOG

To most boaters, fog is fog, but to weather forecasters there are different types of fog including: radiation fog, which forms at night over land and smaller bodies of water; steam fog, which is caused by cold air over warm water; and advection fog, which is caused by warm air over cold water. For boaters, the marine fog that hides buoys, rocks and other boats has only one appropriate strategy—stop.

Fog is a danger to visibility and halts Houston Ship Channel traffic an average of 12 days per year at the Port. Some of the foggiest ports in the world encounter more than 200 days of fog annually.

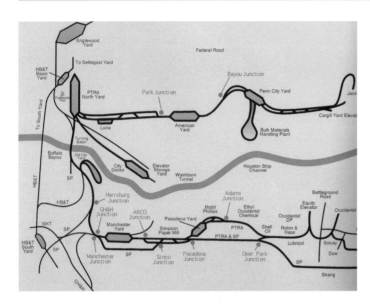

RAILROADS – INTERMODAL TRANSPORTATION

Through-truss swing railroad bridge over Buffalo Bayou near Wayside, with a Union Pacific freight train crossing. Its ability to rotate 90 degrees from center pivot can give tall vessels unobstructed passage.

Whether it floats, flies, or rides by rail, coordination is vital to the Port's ability to move cargo. Activity at Port of Houston Bulk Material Handling Terminal is a model example of intermodal transportation which entails packing cargo in such a way that it can be carried from point of origin to destination without being unpacked and repackaged several times along the way saving valuable time, labor, and storage charges. This concept prompted the design of two types of cargo vessels: ocean going container ships and barge carriers deployed along inland waterways.

BAYPORT CRUISE TERMINAL

The Bayport Cruise Terminal completed in 2007 is an example of beauty and environmental awareness with its aqua tinted glass building and its Leadership in Energy & Environmental Design (LEED) accreditation. Two premier cruise lines, Princess Cruises and Norwegian Cruise Lines, sail from this terminal.

NEW AGE PETROLEUM TERMINAL

Battleground Oil Specialty Terminal Company (BOSTCO) completed the first phase of its almost $500 million project in 2013. This large petroleum storage facility is designed to support the logistical challenges in the black oil market; 52 storage tanks with a capacity 6.2 million barrels will handle residual fuel, feedstocks, distillates, and other petroleum product.

Fingertip hoisting

Closing the hatch to set sail

PEOPLE OF THE PORT

100

Roger Guenther, Port Authority Executive Director, is backed by Port employees.

Cargo commander readies for "pulling" cargo.

Fireboat first response team on deck and in training. To work on a Port of Houston fireboat, a person must be certified as a firefighter and a marine firefighter by State of Texas.

Power rigging for extra-heavy lifts

Captain George Allien, first appointed Branch Pilot, 1916.

Captain Joe Weikerth, commissioned by the governor in 1917 for the Port of Houston and Galveston Bar, with a deck hand aboard the Houston Pilot No 2.

Tugs and boat pilots are the heroes of the channel. Pilots make sure all vessels stay on course through the channel and avoid the occasional natural hazards, like shifting sandbars. The pilot fleet consists of two station boats and two shuttle boats.

Houston pilot, Sherri Hickman, assures safe passage.

HOUSTON PILOTS, "SILENT SERVANTS OF PROGRESS"

Pilotage is a profession as old as sea travel itself, and it is one of the most important in maritime safety. Long ago, pilots directed sea voyages from the beginning to end. Today's pilots have valuable local knowledge they use to skillfully navigate ships through their home ports. A pilot group's mission is to provide safe, reliable, and efficient transits within the port or area they service. Colloquialisms such as: White Hats, Black Hats (on and off Duty), Monkey Fists (a special knot), and Texas Chicken (a traffic procedure) are commonly used by the pilots. In perilous conditions in the Houston Ship Channel pilots frequently say "the bottom was too near the top!"

A member of the Houston Pilots Association concentrates on getting his ship through a tight place.

A Houston Pilot narrows the gap below with an iron grip.

U.S. COAST GUARD AT THE PORT

Fellow Commissioner James T. Edmonds succeeded Ned Holmes as Port Commission Chairman in 2000 and with Tom Kornegay at his port side as Executive Director (Kornegay is the longest tenured Executive Director in Port history serving 17 years of his total 37 Port years in that position), expected to face most of the same issues as his predecessors. Then, the 9/11 tragedy changed lives, procedures, protocol and heightened alert status everywhere, especially at the largest petrochemical complex in the U.S., the Port of Houston. TWIC ID cards were issued and the Houston Ship Channel Security District was formed by the Texas State legislature in a collaborative effort by the private sector on the Port and the Port of Houston Authority to safeguard the Houston Ship Channel.

In 2011, Chairman Edmonds hosts members of the U.S. Homeland Security Subcommittee on this Coast Guard vessel. The Port of Houston's collaborative efforts in regard to security have become a national model.

In addition to round-the-clock focus on security by air through use of cameras, sensors, radar, and other technology, the Coast Guard uses the "chopper" for speed and maneuverability.

High-level strategy plans are made between Captains Woodring and Diehl.

The Coast Guard provides constant surveillance and monitoring along the ship channel to ensure safety and protection.

PORT FIRE BOATS - THEN AND NOW

100

Delivered in 1926, the first fireboat, Port Houston, was ordered by the Houston Fire Commissioner after a fire started in the hold of a steamship carrying cotton.

The Captain Crotty fireboat was put into service in 1950 after safety awareness was heightened from a waterfront explosion that devastated Texas City in 1947. This smaller, faster, and better equipped fireboat was named for the venerable Captain Charles Crotty, an institution in the Navigation District during the first half of the 20th century.

The Howard T. Tellepsen fireboat was christened in 1983 and retired in 2013.

The J. S. Bracewell fireboat was christened in 1983, retired in 2013.

The Port of Houston Authority introduces its Emergency Response Vessel (Fireboat 2) on its way home in 2013. The fleet consists of three high-performance fireboats with a state-of-the-art command center and powerful diesel engines capable of 45 knots, compared to 15 knots of the recently retired fireboats.

BARGES AND TUGBOATS – WORKHORSES OF THE WATERWAYS

Fuel is delivered directly to ships using bunker tank barges. This tug uses its 2,000 horsepower engines to push over 3,500 tons of fuel on a football-field-sized bunker tank barge to one of the scores of ocean-going vessels in need of heavy-diesel fuel. The Port of Houston is home to the nation's busiest petrochemical complex and has no equal with respect to the millions of tons of exports that flow from the dozens of terminals that populate its waterways. Thus, it should come as no surprise that Houston and its adjacent ports handle the greatest number of ships in the country—many of which need fuel before departing to their next destination. This particular fleet of 24 bunker barges is the largest in the U.S. and capable of pumping over 100,000 gallons an hour to facilitate just-in-time commerce.

No holiday respite but plenty of Christmas spirit on this tug pushing product along the Houston Ship Channel.

The labyrinth of barge piping is being coaxed into the Channelview sunset.

The constant push and tow motion moves cargo along its way on the Houston Ship Channel.

NEVER-ENDING DREDGING

Disposal of dredged material began long before the Port was christened in 1914. Originally, much of the dredge material was used to build up banks that eroded due to storms or to create artificial land extensions. Now one of the many uses of the sediment is to build artificial reefs maintained for natural habitat and marshes. One example is the 2005 Mid-Bay Navigation Project that includes 1,100 acres of marsh and upland habitat—part of 4,250 acres of marshland created over the economic life of the project which also includes rebuilding historical islands and development of new oyster reefs. Dredging and widening for larger ships and increasing waterway traffic plays a key role in sustainable development consisting of economic prosperity, environmental stewardship, and social responsibility.

Excavation material displaced by dredging equipment and piping can be effectively used for land reclamation, dike construction, wetland/habitat development, and other beneficial activities. Constant dredging caused by shoaling and sandbars of the 52-mile Houston Ship Channel includes a "groomed" 27-mile pathway through Galveston Bay (average depth of seven feet in the bay) that measures 45 feet deep and 530 feet wide for ship passage and an additional 200 feet wide by 12 feet deep on each side for barge lanes.

Pictured is the imposing business end of a cutterhead dredge. Another hydraulic type, the hopper dredge, is used for large offshore operations. The clamshell or bucket dredges are mechanical dredges that accommodate tight quarters such as next to a dock or quay.

ENVIRONMENTAL MATTERS

Environmental concerns were addressed in innovative ways during the deepening and widening of the Houston Ship Channel that began in 1999. The largest question was centered around the dredging and how to deal with the dredging material—not just from the maintenance dredging but also from the dredging necessary to deepen and widen the main stem in the bay and to make the cut to the new terminal. These weren't the only environmental concerns, but the Port began the process of engaging opponents and addressing concerns. A system of using the dredge material to rebuild reefs and islands in the bay area was born.

Using innovative methods and inventive devices, the Port Authority's Environmental Management System (EMS) program concentrated on reducing air emissions, lessening the impacts of storm water runoff, and increasing recycling. The Port Authority developed and successfully implemented its EMS at Barbours Cut Terminal and Central Maintenance Facility. Both facilities have become the first of any U.S. port facilities to meet the rigorous environmental standards of ISO 14001 compliance. These efforts and the resulting programs ultimately earned the Port of Houston environmental awards.

In 1990, the Beneficial Uses Group (BUG) was formed to develop innovative and beneficial ways dredge material from the Houston Ship Channel could be put to an environmentally friendly use. A 250-acre demonstration marsh was built, which surpassed anything ever attempted in marsh restoration.

Chairman Ned Holmes and Executive Director Tom Kornegay, assisted by an AmeriCorps worker, demonstrate the planting of cordgrass on Atkinson Island in upper Galveston Bay in 1995.

1997 oil skimmer sets out on a test run to clean up oil spills.

Virtually all of the material dredged in the Houston Ship Channel is used to create thousands of acres of marsh and bird habitats. Roots from the plants anchor the dredge material which provides safety and a food center for small fish and marine life.

100

Young adults participate in the Galveston Bay Foundation Marsh Mania planting bundles of smooth cord grass into the muddy ground. This helps to expand the salt marshes that give migrating and native shorebirds, as well as sea life from nearby Galveston Bay, a place to live and raise their young.

Volunteers, including Port SupPORTers, collect debris along a portion of Buffalo Bayou.

Balancing economic progress and environmental sensitivity have become the cornerstone of the Port of Houston. The fruits of prosperity in business with environmental stewardship and education reap rewards beyond expectations.

Volunteers at the Eco Bash *restore vegetation to bayou banks.*

Mighty Tidy *skims litter and debris, providing a solution to the problem of visible pollution that accumulates on Buffalo Bayou.*

School children participate in a 1996 environmental clean up.

100

LADY AT THE HELM

The port's current helmsman, Janiece Longoria, Chairman of the Port Commission, has tech-savvy ideas of her own. Speed of commerce isn't just about trucks, trains, or ships. Chairman Longoria encouraged developing an app that will alert truck drivers if their scheduled pick up is offloaded from a docked ship and ready to roll.

No wheels, no rails, no propellers—just ones and zeros transmitted using radio waves to move cargo more efficiently from sea to land. Another concept floated is a pneumatic tube from Houston to Dallas, in which containers are shuttled back and forth—a cargo pipeline of sorts.

The M/T Lovely Lady pauses dockside on the Houston Ship Channel as product tankers slide past her under the silhouette of the San Jacinto Monument.

2013

Janiece Longoria appointed first woman chairman in Port history

2013

Port introduces most modern fleet of First Response vessels in the world

The overall objective is to speed turn-time, thereby reducing third party wait time—speeding up the trucks or trains ferrying the containers. The payoff will add to the Port's "container throughput" capacity, getting goods in and out of the Port rapidly so that vessels can be offloaded and loaded quicker, resulting in their getting underway faster.

In 1914, Miss Sue Campbell inaugurated Houston's era of deep-water as she cast roses into that part of Buffalo Bayou referred to as the Turning Basin. Her words have been fulfilled over the last century—boats of all nations have come to the Port of Houston and received hearty welcome. And in 2014, again a female hand is launching the Port into the next 100 years of service. Port Commission Chairman Longoria has the vision of her predecessors as well as leadership to secure a promising future. Chairman Longoria also has a concern for the environment.

Her intention is to convert port vehicles to liquefied natural gas (LNG) in order to reduce emissions and utilize fuel harvested in the United States. Dredging is an ongoing function of the Port; after all, the channel has to be maintained and will ultimately be deepened to accommodate bigger ships. She is working with environmental groups, engineering and civil entities to find environmentally useful solutions for the dredge material.

Not unlike her predecessor, Chairman Longoria sees the future of the Port as a cohesive partnership with industry, municipalities, and state governments, as well as labor and environmental groups. Not all are domestic. She acknowledges an interlaced relationship with counterparts around the world. Additionally, there are economic councils, consuls, and academia—all presenting their own needs and challenges.

2013

Princess Cruises' inaugural from Bayport

2013

BOSTCO begins operations at its "greenfield" terminal

2014

Norwegian Cruise Line® inaugural sailing from Bayport

Regardless of the kind of challenge facing the port, solutions have always surfaced from visionary thinking. According to Chairman Longoria, the Port exhibits the power of an idea. That's how the Port began. Centuries ago, George Graham had the notion that the entirety of Galveston Bay would one day be a center for commerce so important that the United States should claim the region. The Cloppers envisioned the unlikely Buffalo Bayou would be a great way to reach the Texas interior in order to establish trade. The Allens foresaw and founded a city with a port 52 miles inland at the junction of two bayous. Thomas Ball, Horace Baldwin Rice, and Jesse Jones agreed with their concept and decided it was time Houston became a deep-water port. Howard Tellepsen employed the idea of partnering with industry to create a huge industrial complex.

These weren't just ordinary ideas. They were bold answers to big challenges supported by a persevering and resolute populace. Undaunted and willpower define the last 100 years. But what's next?

All centennials celebrate achievement, persistence, and durability. The Port of Houston has more than its fair share of high-water marks, as illustrated and noted in this book. The history of the Port is an atypical story of an indomitable vision that simply had to become reality as if it were manifesting destiny. And looking forward, as the Port's potential for greater cargo capacity is still on the horizon —it enjoys a rare position in handling break-bulk, dry-bulk, and liquid-bulk that continues to strengthen its promising future. So much of that promise was made a short 100 years ago when, as the Port grew, the city also grew and as the Port prospered, so prospered the city. But if all history is prologue, then perhaps a quote by one of Houston's 1920s era industrial giants was actually prophetic. Timber titan, John Henry Kirby once said of the Port of Houston, "Why, my friends, we are only getting started..."

The waterway distance from the Turning Basin to Main Street Houston is 6.5 miles and 4 miles point-to-point. Some of the disconnect between the typical Houstonian and the Port is attributed to the Port's "geographical isolation." Nonetheless the Port's value as the prevailing economic catalyst of Houston is irreplaceable and separates Houston from other major cities.

2014
Port celebrates its centennial

THE PORT OF HOUSTON AUTHORITY

Janiece M. Longoria
Chairman

The city of Houston and the Harris County Commissioners Court each appoint two commissioners. These two government entities jointly appoint the chairman of the Port Commission. The Harris County Mayors & Councils Association, representing 26 cities, and the city of Pasadena each appoint one commissioner.

John D. Kennedy
Commissioner

Dean E. Corgey
Commissioner

Clyde Fitzgerald
Commissioner

Theldon R. Branch, III
Commissioner

Stephen H. DonCarlos
Commissioner

Roy D. Mease
Commissioner

1914 ◁—⊗—▷ 2014

The Port Authority is an autonomous governing body authorized by an act of the Texas State Legislature in 1909 and approved by voters of Harris County in 1910 as the Harris County Houston Ship Channel Navigation District. The name was changed to the Port of Houston Authority in 1971.

VISION

The Port of Houston Authority serves as the maritime gateway to Texas and the heartland of America by leading in global commerce, environmental stewardship, community focus and economic prosperity.

MISSION

The Port of Houston Authority facilitates commerce, navigation, and safe waterways promoting sustainable trade and generating economic development for the Houston region, Texas, and the nation, while being a model environmental and security steward, and a community-focused and fiscally responsible organization.

TIMELINE

1836 – Texas Independence from Mexico

Brothers Augustus Chapman Allen and John Kirby Allen found Houston

Houston becomes temporary capital of Texas

1837 – The *Laura* was 1st steamship on Buffalo Bayou

1840 – Wharf built from Main to Fannin

1841 – City Ordinance establishing Port of Houston

1845 – Texas becomes the 28th state in the Union

1870 – Congress designates Houston a port

1876 – The *Clinton* was the 1st ocean steamship to call

1895 – Houston receives heaviest snowfall on record. Over 20 inches buries the city and does not melt for days

1896 – Tom Ball begins term as Congressman

Congress Rivers and Harbors Committee approves survey of Houston Ship Channel from Galveston Island to Houston

1899 – Houston's first park opens. The site, now Sam Houston Park, contains several of Houston's earliest buildings

1900 – Great Storm devastates Galveston Island

City of Houston population at 63,800

1901 – First oil gusher comes in at Spindletop

1902 – Congress appropriates dredging funds for Houston Ship Channel

1903 – Wright Brothers, first to fly

1907 – Ship Channel dredged to 18.5 foot depth

1909 – Houston Plan adopted by Congress to finance channel improvements

1911– Harris County Houston Ship Channel Navigation District created

"Houston Plan" Bond approved by 16-1 margin

1912 – *Titanic* sinks

Rice Institute founded

Houston Ship Channel Route altered

1913 – Houston Symphony established

1914 – The Port is christened with "Deep-Water Jubilee"

The *Dorothy* arrives at Port with cargo of coal

World War I begins

Panama Canal opens

Hermann Park opens

USS Texas is launched

Sam Houston Area Council of the Boy Scouts established

Rotary Club founded

1915 – Gulf hurricane strikes the area

The *Satilla* arrival marks the official opening of the Port of Houston

RMS Lusitania sunk by German U-boat

Houston pilots appointed by governor

1917 – United States enters World War I

Camp Logan and Ellington Field built

1918 – Armistice declared

First Refinery built on Houston Ship Channel

30 industrial facilities line banks of Buffalo Bayou

1919 – *S.S. Merry Mount*, first ship bound for Europe, leaves the Port

1920 – Port of Houston becomes 6th largest in U.S.

1921 – Cotton annual transports almost 500,000 bales

1922 – Unification of City Harbors Board and Harris County Houston Ship Channel Navigation District

Upgrades to public docks and Long Reach docks begin

1923 – Pilots under the control of the Port

1924 – Port Terminal Railroad organized

Memorial Park Opens

1925 – Port launches its first fireboat, *Port Houston*

Public Grain Elevator is built at Turning Basin

1928 – Port introduces *RJ Cummins*, its first inspection boat

1929 – Cotton annual transports 2 million bales

Wall Street crashes and the Great Depression begins

1930 – Grain tonnage reaches 5 million bushels

Refining capacity reaches 3.25 million barrels/month

Twenty-seven oil tankers service refineries at the port

USS Houston visits Port of Houston

1932 – Port handles 2.97 million bushels of grain

Jesse H. Jones becomes chairman of Reconstruction Finance Corp

1933 – Lights installed along Houston Ship Channel allowing night navigation

1934 – Ship arrivals reach 2,500 carrying 19.3 million tons of cargo

Intracoastal Canal System links Houston with the Mississippi River system of navigation

Houston becomes oil refining capital of the world

University of Houston became a four-year institution

1935 – Depression relief for Houstonians reaches more than $8 million

1936 – Texas and Houston celebrate Centennials

FDR tours Port of Houston, declares it "vital"

Freight tonnage reaches 30 million

Port of Houston ranked first in the South

Houston Port and Traffic Bureau established

1937 – Port of Houston ranked second behind NY in tonnage

Houston Municipal Airport, which would later become William P. Hobby Airport, is opened

Port Houston exports scrap metal to Japan

Japan invades China

1939 – San Jacinto Battleground Monument opens to public

Freight tonnage reaches 30 million

Germany launches Blitzkrieg

1940 – Jesse Jones becomes Secretary of Commerce

City of Houston population at 384,500

Houston dismantled the last of its streetcar system

1941 – Japan attacks United States at Pearl harbor

1942 – German U-boats prowl Gulf of Mexico

USS Houston sunk in the Pacific

1943 – Synthetic rubber was mass produced for the first time by two new Houston area plants and shipped for use in World War II through the Port of Houston.

Wartime industries in full swing along Houston Ship Channel

1944 – Bond approved to build Washburn and Baytown Tunnels

1945 – World War II ends with surrender of Germany and Japan

1947 – Texas City explosion

Houston voters defeat the first-ever referendum for citywide zoning

Sam Houston I inspection boat replaces *RJ Cummins*

1948 – The Gulf Freeway, Texas' first freeway opens as U.S. Highway 75, signaling the beginning of freeway construction in the city

Value of tonnage passing through the Port reaches $1 billion

1950 – Houston ranked second in U.S. for total tonnage

Fireboat, *Capt Crotty*, launched at Port

Washburn Tunnel completed

1952 – Port of Houston acquired land at Barbours Cut

1953 – Baytown Tunnel opened to public

1954 – Greater Houston Metropolitan area reaches 1 million population

1956 – First container ship, *Ideal X* arrives in Houston with 58 containers

$7 million bond issue passed by 68%

Port acquires Long Reach docks (Turning Basin)

1957 – Port expands intra-railroad network

1958 – Port launches the *M/V Sam Houston II* (current tour boat)

TIMELINE

1961 – NASA moves headquarters to Houston/Clear Lake

Hurricane Carla struck the Texas Coast

Bulk Handling Plant Terminal completed

1962 – World Trade Center opens in downtown Houston

1963 – The Humble Building completed, then the tallest building west of the Mississippi River

1964 – 50th anniversary of Port of Houston

Port announces purchase of major portion of Bayport property

136 million bushels of grain moves through the Port

Tonnage reaches 60 million valued at $4 billion

1965 – The Astrodome opens as the 8th wonder of the world

Port purchases Long Reach Docks

First container crane in the Gulf Coast delivered to Houston

1969 – *Apollo 11* lands on the moon

"Houston" is first word spoken from the lunar surface

Houston Intercontinental Airport, now named George H. W. Bush Intercontinental Airport, is opened to the public

1971 – Port of Houston Authority becomes official title

Shell Oil Company relocates corporate headquarters to Houston. More than 200 major firms move headquarters, subsidiaries and divisions here in the years following

1972 – Barbours Cut Lash Dock operations open

1973 – The Arab Oil Embargo causes demand for Texas oil to boom.

Houston International Seafarers Center opens at Turning Basin

Sidney Sherman Bridge (610 Bridge over Turning Basin) opens

1974 – Bayport Channel dedication

1977 – Barbours Cut begins container terminal operations

1981 – Kathryn J. Whitmire is elected as the first woman mayor of Houston

Double stack train container transport began in Houston

1982 – Beltway 8 Bridge (Jesse H. Jones Memorial Bridge) opens

1983 – Hurricane Alicia hits Houston and Galveston

Free Trade Zones (FTZ) established throughout the Port

1984 – Wharf Number 32 completed at Turning Basin

1989 – Jacintoport Terminal opened featuring its Spiralveyor

Port of Houston 8th busiest port in the world

Port of Houston is 1st in foreign tonnage in U.S.

1990 – The Beneficial Uses Group (BUG) was formed to develop environmentally innovative and beneficial ways to use dredge material from the Houston Ship Channel

Houston hosts the 16th G7 Summit.

1991 – The Port ranks the third-largest load center for the U.S. military during the Gulf War

New Port of Houston Authority Building opened at Turning Basin

1992 – Public Elevator No. 2 opened with 6.2 million bushel capacity

1993 – Lou Lawler Seafarers Center opened in La Porte

Woodhouse Terminal acquired by the Port

Port announces purchase of additional Bayport property

City zoning defeated for the third time

1995 – Fred Hartman Bridge opened to public

Care Terminal acquired by the Port

1997 – Baytown Tunnel removed

Barbours Cut Cruise Terminal opens

1999 – Port reaches milestone 1 million TEUs (containers) per year

Bond approved for first phase at Bayport Terminals

2001 – Following 9/11, Port initiates industry-leading security measures

Tropical Storm Allison causes widespread flooding in the Houston area. The storm is called a 500-year event

2003 – Norwegian Cruise Line sails from Barbours Cut

2004 – First modern light rail line (7.5 miles) begins operations

  Port Authority sought out and received federal security grants and opened the Port Coordination Center to enhance communication

2005 – Houston Ship Channel completes 30 year project: 530' wide, 45' deep

  Hurricane Katrina devastates New Orleans

2007 – Houston Ship Channel Security District authorized by Texas State Legislature

2007 – $250 million Bond issue passed by 65% vote

  Bayport Container Terminal begins operations

2008 – Hurricane Ike hits Houston and Galveston

  Bayport Cruise Terminal Building opens to assist after Hurricane Ike

  World's first port certified ISO 28000:2007 for security management

2010 – Pilots add *Yellow Rose* to fleet of vessels

2013 – Janiece Longoria appointed first woman chairman in Port history

  Port introduces most modern fleet of First Response vessels in the world

  Princess Cruises' inaugural sailing from Bayport

  BOSTCO begins operations at its "greenfield" terminal

2014 – Norwegian Cruise Line® inaugural sailing from Bayport

2014 – Port celebrates centennial

THE HOUSTON SHIP CHANNEL DELIVERS FIRST AND FOREMOST

The Houston Ship Channel was first federal project to have a local match component to it. In 1909, Houston Mayor Horace Baldwin Rice and U.S. Congressman Tom Ball presented the "Houston Plan" to the U.S. House of Representatives Rivers and Harbors Committee. Congress approved it, and every port constructed in the U.S. since 1910 has followed this concept which guarantees local financial support.

The first direct shipment of cotton to Europe was 23,719 bales that left the Port of Houston in November 1919 on the *S.S. Merry Mount*.

In 1920, the first director of the port, Benjamin Casey Allin, III, developed and subsequently patented an industrial site and railway access design that remains in popular use today by ports and other industries. His warehouse and wharf shed design features a spur of the main railway line running through it so that rail cars can be loaded and unloaded without delaying traffic on the mainline.

In 1937, the Port of Houston reached the status of second only to New York in tonnage and importance, according to *Fortune Magazine*. Its position slipped slightly during World War II, but by 1948, the Port of Houston was once again number two in overall tonnage.

Synthetic rubber was mass produced for the first time in 1943 by two new Houston area plants and shipped for use in World War II through the Port of Houston.

After World War II, development of the petrochemical industry along the Houston Ship Channel accelerated until the Port of Houston became home to the nation's largest petrochemical production complex and second largest in the world.

Containerization was born when the world's first container ship, *M/V Ideal X*, sailed with 58 containers from New York/New Jersey on April 26, 1956 and unloaded five days later at the Port of Houston.

Developed by the Port of Houston Authority in 1962, the Houston World Trade Building was the first ever to be built as a focal point for world trade activity of a port and community. It was designed as a central location for international trade interests including consular offices, transportation companies, importers and exporters.

In 1962, Houston became the first choice of the National Aeronautics and Space Administration (NASA) as the site of its new headquarters for the manned space

program partially due to the fact that Houston's ship channel and port facilities provided an excellent means for transporting bulky space vehicles.

In 1966, the first container crane in the U.S. Gulf of Mexico was installed at the Houston Ship Channel.

Use of the double-stack train was introduced at the Port of Houston in 1981. By placing one container on top of another, transportation costs were greatly reduced.

Also in 1990, the Beneficial Users Group (BUG) was formed to address how the dredge material from the Houston Ship Channel could be put to an environmentally friendly use. A 250-acre demonstration marsh was built, which surpassed anything ever attempted in marsh restoration. Over the 50-year life of the deepening and widening project, an unprecedented 4,250 acres of marsh, a six-acre bird island, the 3,000-foot long Goat Island, and Redfish Island will be built.

The Port of Houston is No. 1 in foreign waterborne tonnage in the U.S. in 1996 and has retained that title for nearly 20 consecutive years.

In 1996, the Port of Houston became the first U.S. port with a multi-site Disposal Area Management Program (DAMP).

Originally built in 1953, the Baytown Tunnel had to be removed in 1997 as a part of the deepening and widening of the Houston Ship Channel. Houston became the first port to remove a tunnel of this magnitude (35' diameter by 1,041' in length) without closing the ship channel, lost time accidents, or navigational safety impacts.

The Port of Houston first joined the 1 million container club in 1999 when it moved 1,001,170 TEUs that year.

Named the 4th U.S. Green Coffee Port in 2003.

Selected as "The Irreplaceable Port" in 2012 by *Colliers International White Paper*.

Railway Industrial Clearance Association (RICA) Award in 2013 for the second time.

Colliers International recognized the Port in 2013 with the "Gulf's Darn Profitable" (GDP) Award.

In 2013, Janiece Longoria became the first female to become Chairman of the Port of Houston Authority.

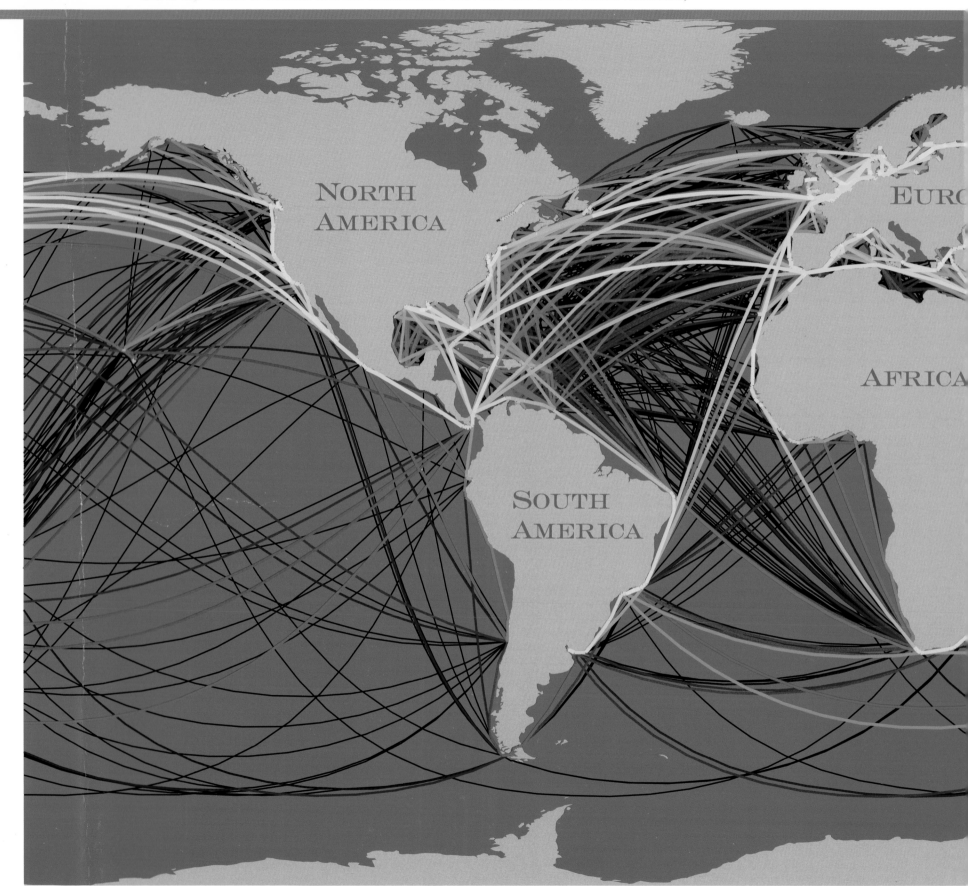

70% OF THE WORLD IS COVERED IN WATER,
80% OF THE WORLD'S POPULATION LIVES ON OR NEAR WATER,